THE
NUMISMATIST'S BEDSIDE
COMPANION

THE
NUMISMATIST'S BEDSIDE COMPANION

VOLUME ONE
EDITED BY Q. DAVID BOWERS

PUBLISHED BY BOWERS AND MERENA GALLERIES, INC.

ISBN 0-943161-02-9

Published by:
Bowers and Merena Galleries, Inc.
Box 1224, Wolfeboro, NH 03894

The cover design is by Elli Ford of Jungle Graphics, Center Sandwich, New Hampshire, and was inspired by a cartoon, "The Numismatist's Dream," by Verkler, in *The Numismatist* in 1907.

Table of Contents

Introduction

By Q. David Bowers

W hile the primary purpose of the *Rare Coin Review,* the illustrated magazine issued by Bowers and Merena Galleries, is to sell rare coins, over the years hundreds of research articles, news items, stories, and interesting fillers have graced its pages. The mix has been an attractive one to readers, as evidenced by a letter I received in 1986 in which the sender expressed the desire to exchange his check for $500 for a complete set of *Rare Coin Review* issues. Unfortunately, the request could not be filled.

Typically, the circulation of the *Rare Coin Review* has been in the range of 10,000 to 20,000, with a few issues exceeding the latter number. For example, one issue was sent on a trial basis to 15,000 or so readers of *The Coin Dealer Newsletter,* in addition to those on our own mailing list. In every instance, however, the *Rare Coin Review* has been produced in a quantity determined by the number of people on our mailing list, additional requests on hand, and perhaps an extra 500 to 1,000 for sample mailing and requests received between issues. Like many other numismatic publications, the *Rare Coin Review* is of an ephemeral nature. When No. 66 came out, the contents of No. 65 were forgotten, and perhaps the earlier copy was tossed out by the typical reader. In any event, a number of issues have become scarce, and it is not at all unusual for numismatic booksellers to charge $5 to $10 for single early copies. Book dealer Cal Wilson told me that he once sold a single copy of a rare early issue for $115!

As editor and primary author of the *Rare Coin Review* I have enjoyed the publication immensely. While each issue has pulled its weight from the standpoint of orders for coins received, a far greater satisfaction has been the enjoyment expressed in countless letters from readers.

Over the years there have been numerous counterparts to the *Rare Coin Review,* beginning with Ed. Frossard's controversial *Numisma* house organ published in the late 1870s and 1880s. Frossard delighted his readers with articles, gossip, frank evaluations of his competitors (in an era when those aggrieved were not as eager to sue as they are now), and a generous helping of research information. *Mehl's Numismatic Monthly,* issued by famous Texas dealer, B. Max Mehl, gave *The Numismatist,* the official journal of the American Numismatic Association, a run for its money when it was published during the early part of the present century. In later years, Stack's *Numismatic Review,* published in the 1940s, and *Numisma,* issued by the New Netherlands Coin Company in the 1950s, delighted readers.

But there are several problems with these and other early article-filled house organs. First, copies today are quite scarce. Second, they were discontinued after relatively short publication spans. The reality of economics probably intervened. Like it or not, on a page-for-page basis, the *Special Coin Letter,* issued by Bowers and Merena Galleries, a concise eight-page price list without any articles, sells a lot more coins. As profit is supposed to be the bottom line of any commercial operation, logic dictates the *Rare Coin Review* should be discontinued and the gap should be filled with more *Special Coin Letter* emissions. However, I have always *enjoyed* producing the *Rare Coin Review,* and as an owner of the company, I suppose that is sufficient reason for publishing it; no financial justification is necessary! If ours was a publicly owned company, and every dollar had to count, perhaps shareholders would complain and we would discontinue the *Rare Coin Review.* But, as it is, the *Rare Coin Review* lives on—with pages devoted to research information, numismatic articles both basic and obscure, and other things which I find interesting and which, in general, contribute to the indefinable spirit of numismatics.

The present publication, *The Numismatist's Bedside Companion,* is a compendium of over two dozen articles which appeared in the *Rare Coin Review* from 1970 through 1985. Some are reprints of articles from early sources, with those by Frank M. Todd, George F. Dow, and, obviously, Mark Twain fitting in that category. Others are by well-known writers of our own time, including Dennis Loring, D'Arcy O'Connor, Walter Breen, Bruce Lorich, James F. Ruddy, and David L. Ganz. The remaining articles bear my byline.

The subjects covered are diverse. You will read about the 1856 Flying Eagle cent, one of America's most popular rarities. The Oak Island treasure, one of the greatest unsolved mysteries of pirate days, is the subject of another article, while some queer doings in a Nevada silver mine are the subject of another. Numismatic terminology (what does "excessively rare" mean?), the psychology of collecting, the sentimental story of a girl who had some rare gold dollars, a coin auction held in 1870, nostrums such as Moxie and Drake's Plantation Bitters, and even a numismatic horoscope are among the topics of articles—to mention just a few.

The cover features an original work of art by Elli Ford, a talented artist who makes her home in Center Sandwich, New Hampshire, and was inspired by a cartoon sketch by Verkler, which appeared in *The Numismatist* in 1907. It is presumed, of course, that the serious numismatist does nothing but eat, drink, and sleep coins! Of course, we all know that this is not true—but we all know at the same time, that the pursuit of coins and the reading of interesting stories about them makes life all the more enjoyable.

So, take this first volume in our *Numismatist's Bedside Companion* series to bed with you, fluff up your favorite pillow, and settle down to some interesting reading before you turn out the light.

—Q. David Bowers
October 21, 1987

Some Ramblings About Writing

| By Q. David Bowers | 1985 |

*T*he following article is adapted from a talk given at a fund-
raising event sponsored by the Friends of the Wolfeboro
(New Hampshire) Library, Thursday afternoon, May 30, 1985. Four
different authors were invited to the event—to tell how they got
started, and "what it is like to be a writer."

Writing is a form of self expression, and I guess I have always liked
to express myself. I am sure that I made my opinions known at a very
early age, but an event that particularly sticks in my mind—from the
vantage point of many years later—is a debate in which I was involved
back in 1951 as a seventh grader in the Forty Fort (Pennsylvania) High
School.

My English teacher, Miss Lorraine Rice, thought it would be nice if
some of the seventh graders formed a debating team. As luck would
have it, I was appointed captain. The subject of a memorable debate
had to do with the Strategic Air Command, and whether or not B-36
bombers should be kept aloft day and night so that on a moment's
notice they could head for Russia—and, equally important, whether
these and other large aircraft were worth the prices taxpayers had to
pay for them. This, of course, was before the missile age, and I now
suspect that even the cheapest military missile now would probably
buy a whole flock of B-36s!

I don't remember which side I was on—pro or con—but I do
remember that I gave what Miss Rice thought was a "brilliant" perform-

ance. Apparently, unlike a number of my classmates, I really dug into the subject beforehand. I wrote to the Convair Aircraft Company in San Diego, California, to get information on the B-36. I wrote to Boeing in Seattle to get data on their planes. I asked the government for information, and I went to the library. So, when the debate came, I was very well equipped.

After discussing the matter within my own class, Miss Rice proposed that my team debate the high school seniors. We did this, and, believe it or not, the audience felt that my team of seventh graders was the winner! This gave me quite a bit of self confidence and a nice ego boost. At the time I was rather shy socially, so perhaps this debating prowess made up for it in my own mind—and gave me a sense of accomplishment.

The next year, when I was in eighth grade, I was invited to address the assembled students of Forty Fort High School on Washington's Birthday. Back then we all believed, falsely it turned out, that the Father of our Country was born on February 22. Now we all know that he was born on the third Monday of February! Anyway, faced with giving a solo program to 300 or more students, I decided to do some research. Most of the audience knew, I presumed, that George Washington was the first president of the United States, that he lived at Mount Vernon, and that he distinguished himself in the Revolutionary War. So, by delving into some biographies, I came up with some lesser-known facts; at least they were not well known to me.

I discovered and subsequently related to my audience that the famous cherry tree incident—"Father, I cannot tell a lie—I cut it down—" had no basis in fact but, instead, was a figment of the vivid imagination of one Parson Weems, who created the story for children. I also discovered—shades of naughtiness—that rum was distilled right on Washington's own plantation, and, even more revealing, that in earlier times slaves had been kept there. I told of a few dozen other obscure facts, some which I thought were "good things" and others which were "bad." All, I felt, were entertaining.

The audience loved it, and I received long and loud applause. I was on cloud nine, until the next day when I was called into the principal's office and was told that he had received quite a bit of criticism concerning my talk. It seems as though students in the audience went home and related their newfound knowledge to their parents. The principal, Leon Bubeck, was then telephoned by angry parents who protested the debunking of our national hero.

"I know that you didn't do any debunking," Mr. Bubeck assured me, "so don't worry about anything that you hear. I am sure that if these parents had been there they would have enjoyed the speech as much as I did."

That may have been my first confrontation with controversy—a subject to which I have been no stranger since. Anyway, I remember the seventh grade debating team and the eighth grade George Washington speech as early self-expressions which influenced me greatly. Both showed that some research would result in a presentation that would bring new knowledge to listeners, or, later, readers.

Forty Fort High School, a two-story brick-faced structure, was hardly a fancy place. Audiovisual equipment was at a minimum, facilities were rather sparse, and the surroundings were anything but elegant—at least in comparison to some of the well-funded schools I was later to visit as an adult in Los Angeles and other communities. Believe it or not, the high school students respected the faculty, behaved themselves, drugs were unheard of, and the naughtiest thing anyone was apt to do was to smoke a cigarette in the boy's room or, perhaps on a Friday night take a clandestine sip of beer.

Cigarette smoking and beer drinking interested me not, nor did they in later years, so I did not indulge in even these secret pleasures. We all had a good time. What became the Class of '56 was a close-knit group of nearly 60 people, of diverse interests and abilities, who enjoyed what they were doing and where they were heading. Similarly, the faculty was composed of hard-working, dedicated people who did their best to provide a good education for the students who attended. I am sure that such later-day situations as going on strike were not even dreamed of back then. And, perhaps we were better off the way things were in "the good old days."

It was with some sadness a few years ago that I revisited Forty Fort High School—this was around 1975—to note that the entire Wyoming Valley school district in that northeastern section of Pennsylvania had been consolidated, and that what once was a high school comprising six different grades drawing from students in the immediate surrounding area now was a building filled with many different classes, all of the seventh grade, drawing people from dozens of miles away. I didn't tarry long enough to investigate, but I suspect that something had been lost in the sense of the close-knit feeling that earlier students had. Indeed, the glass showcase filled with old Forty Fort High School athletic and scholastic trophies had been emptied of what I remembered viewing as treasures when I was a kid. Perhaps they are gathering dust in some storeroom.

Lorraine Rice, my English teacher, liked words and encouraged the use of them. In one instance I remember she gave the "words for the week"—10 new vocabulary words to learn. I felt proud of myself when I was able to compose some unwieldly sentence which contained each and every one of the words! And then there were spelling bees. Believe it or not, I have never lost a spelling bee. Before the present reader thinks this is a great accomplishment, I hasten to add that I have never engaged in any spelling bee outside of various high school English classes—perhaps I would have been quickly demolished had I gone further. But, within my own high school English class, I did just fine.

I recall that after winning one spelling bee, Lorraine Rice decided she would keep giving me harder and harder words until at last I had to sit down. I remained standing through a succession of words until *palatial* came up—I spelled it as *palacial*. I have never forgotten that.

At my own office, Bowers and Merena Galleries, we give a spelling quiz to prospective applicants. I have always felt that to give a list of easy words would not accomplish much, so I cannot resist throwing in some toughies. See if you can spell them correctly! If you can, then you are a rare, rare person. Try these:

Moccasin, asinine, sacrilegious, wherewithal, Tennessee.

How well did you do? I am sure that years ago I would have been stumped by sacrilegious, which has an unfair twist to it.

I grew to like words immensely—I still like them today—and whenever I come across a word that I do not know, I look it up. Sometimes I use a word incorrectly. For a number of years I believed that *erstwhile* meant "desirable" or "highly favored." For example, to me it would have been very appropriate to say of a current employee: "I would like you to meet John, my erstwhile business associate." What I meant to convey was that I proposed introducing John, a highly-valued member of our team. What I was really saying was: "I would like you to meet John, a *former* member of our organization!" By the time that I learned that *erstwhile* meant *former* I probably had used it the wrong way a couple of dozen times.

Somewhat similar is the word *penultimate*. I don't recall ever using it in print or in a talk—it was one of those words that I would come across occasionally but never use—but I thought that it meant "ultimate" or "at the top of the heap." Then I learned that *penultimate* meant "next to last." For example, while 1945 was the last year of

World War II, 1944 was the *penultimate* year.

Not only have I enjoyed words, I have enjoyed facts—including miscellaneous information which in recent years has become known as trivia. I don't claim to be an expert on trivia—far from it. In fact, in the *Trivial Pursuit* game I can do just fine in such subjects as history and geography, but I would be an absolute flop if selected as a partner on such subjects as sports and entertainment. So, my accumulation of trivia—not to mention obscure words—is not in all areas or disciplines.

I have always felt that the more information one can get, the better. For *The Numismatist,* the American Numismatic Association's publication for coin collectors, I recently wrote an article, "Overfeeding the Mind," which suggested that there was no such thing as too much knowledge on any subject. I have always felt that if I had 1,000 facts, it would be a snap to write an article with 100 facts in it. However, if I had just 10 facts, if I desired to write even a semi-authoritative article with a few dozen facts in it, I would fall short of the mark and would turn out a mushy, boring product—an article of little use or interest to anyone.

The accumulation of miscellaneous facts takes many forms, but perhaps my favorite way is through old books. I often spend weekends poking around New England visiting old bookstores—that is, stores which sell old books—of which there are dozens of nice ones within a couple hundred mile radius of my home, an area which encompasses all of New Hampshire, a good bit of Vermont, a nice section of Maine (a particularly delightful state for the book hunter!), and quite a bit of Massachusetts. On a recent sortie, I came back with volumes covering such eclectic and varied subjects as the inside story of New York City during the last part of the century, the Free Soil Party of 1848, several volumes on Lafayette, P.T. Barnum writing about wild animals, the bookstore of George Evans in Philadelphia during the last century, the Erie Canal, *A Waif Caught in the Conflict Between Two Civilizations* (a delightful volume by Augustin Thompson—one I have been searching for for a long, long time, and for which I would have gladly paid $200, but it cost me just $20 when I found it!), life in the Massachusetts Bay Colony, the correspondence of Gouverneur Morris, and a couple dozen other things.

All such books are dutifully added to my library, which continues to grow at an alarming rate. Quite a few of these books help me when I write coin articles or coin books, others help when I do books on other subjects (past efforts have included antiques, old cars, music boxes, artists and illustrators, and the beverage Moxie), while still others are simply for enjoyment—I may never use them for serious research.

As a writer, my intellectual curiosity is probably my greatest asset, some small ability to string words together is another asset, and certainly my library is still another. My own library suffices for much numismatic research, still it often becomes necessary to go elsewhere. Recently I borrowed a whole pile of books from the Widener Library in Harvard, and on numerous occasions I have filled out call slips in the halls of the Library of Congress in Washington. In a numismatic vein, Nancy Green, the capable and cheery ANA librarian, has often sent me books on loan or Xeroxes of things that she and her staff have dug out—a nice ANA service which, of course, is available to all ANA members.

Sometimes research turns up interesting things. While delving into the subject of Moxie for my *Moxie Encyclopedia* book, a volume of 760 pages published by the Vestal Press, I noted that current advertising for Moxie often emphasized the slogan "Since 1884." Indeed, in August 1984 a Moxie "centennial" celebration was held. However, in digging into historical information I learned from old ledgers that the first Moxie was sold in March 1885, a year later than most people thought. Checking further, I found that The Moxie Nerve Food Company (as the firm was known until 1909, when it dropped the "Nerve Food" from its name) used the "Since 1885"—or correct—version in its advertising until about 1920, at which time it mysteriously changed to 1884! Whether this was a result of a typographical error which was compounded or what the idea was, I don't know. However, the 1884 error has been perpetuated. My new book straightens out the affair, but I hasten to note in the book that it is possible that Moxie may have been *privately* compounded in 1884.

When I completed my 1,008-page *Encyclopedia of Automatic Musical Instruments* in 1972, I envisioned that 1,000 copies would be sold during the next decade. At least that's what I told the publisher. Now, in 1985, over 15,000 copies are in print—not bad for a $45 book! When I checked my old passport stamps in 1972, as the *Encyclopedia* was nearing completion, I noted that I had been to Europe 27 times. Many of these trips were spent chasing rare coins, but I often had time to track down data concerning old-time orchestrions (self-playing pianos with drums, xylophones, and other things added), music boxes, and the like, including numerous interviews with old-timers once connected with the industry in England, Belgium, Holland,

France, Germany, and elsewhere.

In particular, I remember many conversations I had with Eugene DeRoy—which I mention today as an evidence that not all research comes from libraries or books. Some of the most interesting research, including that I have done concerning numismatic personalities, comes from interviews. In the instance of Mr. DeRoy, I queried him about his activities years ago when he used to make coin-operated pianos and produce music rolls for use on these instruments. Later, during the late 1930s and early 1940s, by which time that industry had faded, he engaged in the repair of old pipe organs, orchestrions, and the like. A delightful old man, Eugene DeRoy regaled me with many tales of years earlier. Particularly poignant were his recollections of life under the Nazis. As you undoubtedly know, Belgium was overrun by Nazis around 1940, after which time much of the adult working population was enslaved to produce machines and other things for the German war effort.

Adolph Hitler proclaimed that *kultur* was alive and well in the Third Reich, and toward this end certain people, even those in enslaved nations, who had abilities in the line of art, music, engraving, or other specialties were often spared from the cruelties or death accorded to others. Eugene DeRoy was recognized as a competent repairer of orchestrions, circus organs, and the like, so he was told to report for work in Germany and to go from place to place repairing instruments still in existence. DeRoy secretly signed up with the Belgian underground movement and formed a liaison by which he became a spy for the Allies, at the risk of death, of course. He would make long trips into Germany, as he was supposed to, returning occasionally to nearby Belgium, where he would visit his wife and daughter and go to a local movie. In the theatre, by prearrangement, he would sit next to another underground agent and relay information to him—information which helped the Allies' cause.

DeRoy, who journeyed extensively through Germany on railroads, the only way he was permitted to travel, made detailed notes of German train schedules, observing when freight and passenger trains came and went to Frankfurt, Berlin, Dusseldorf, Munich, and other places. This information was very valuable to the Allies, for obviously, in a bombing raid it would be more desirable to strike a railroad station if one or more trains were there—instead of having empty tracks and little on the loading dock. After the war, DeRoy received a commendation from the Belgian government. But, so far as I know, except for mention of him in my *Encyclopedia of Automatic Musical Instruments,* his daring exploits have never been recorded.

In another instance, DeRoy, who enjoyed a good glass of beer (or two or three) and didn't want to work any harder than he had to for the Germans, was told to visit a military officers' club which had a dance hall attached. There on one side of the dance hall was a large orchestrion measuring about 12 feet wide by 10 feet high, with all sorts of tubes, pipes, bellows, pumps, and other gadgets on the inside. There was a problem: the thing was silent; it didn't work. DeRoy was commanded to fix it.

He looked at the instrument, studied it with mock concern, and quickly observed that the only real problem was that a piece of tubing had slipped from its connecting joint, thus permitting air pressure to escape, rendering the air-operated instrument silent. However, his German captors, who had not even looked at the inside of the instrument, didn't know the situation was this simple. Scratching his head, DeRoy sorrowfully reported that the orchestrion was in truly sad shape and that it would require a complete overhaul. Eager to get the unit operating once again, the Germans gave DeRoy a comfortable room, all the beer he could drink, and kept him around the officers' club in comfortable circumstances for the next six months! What they didn't know, of course, was that DeRoy made detailed notes concerning every conversation he heard! In the meantime he took the orchestrion apart and then put it back together again—fixing the simple broken connection in the process. When he was finished the instrument worked perfectly, and all were satisfied.

Ever since my first book, *Coins and Collectors,* was written in 1963, right down to some of the recent ones—including *The Moxie Encyclopedia, The Compleat Coin Collector,* and *U.S. Nickel Three-Cent and Five-Cent Pieces*—I have enjoyed writing. In fact, I enjoyed writing long before 1963. In the process I have turned out over two dozen books and well over 1,000 articles. Writing has been a great adventure, and I look forward to many more years of the same, knowing that next year and the year after will bring still more obscure facts, some unimportant, others trivial—but hopefully all of an interesting nature.

The rewards of a writer are many. Strangely, monetary rewards are unimportant. I have no delusion that my 760-page *Moxie Encyclopedia* will be financially worthwhile. Indeed, if one were to add up all the time I spent on it, I probably would not earn even 10 cents an hour. The same goes for most of my coin books. Far more financially rewarding it would have been, in my opinion, to have spent the best part of a summer writing catalogues of coins for sale rather than the book *Virgil Brand: The Man and His Era, Profile of a Numismatist.* But, it was Virgil who I chose to write about, and I have no regrets. Never mind that the book will not be on the best-seller list. A writer's reward is a nice review—or a pat on the head—or the opportunity to share with others—or in the present instance, the invitation of the Friends of the Wolfeboro Library which has given me the opportunity to speak to you today.

From Rare Coin Review *No. 57, Autumn 1985.*

I Don't Touch the Hard Stuff

| By Q. David Bowers | 1984 |

I have in front of me as I write this article a common, yet curious, numismatic item: an 1862 encased postage stamp bearing on the front a pinkish three-cent stamp beneath a sheet of clear mica. To the left and right are two tabs or scallops which are part of a brass frame. Turning the piece over, I read on the reverse the puzzling inscription S.T.1860.X, beneath which is DRAKE'S PLANTATION BIT-TERS, the patent date of August 12, 1862, and the name of J. Gault.

Before exploring the inscription further, it is appropriate to tell a bit about encased postage stamps in general. During the Civil War it was not certain whether the Union or the Confederacy would be the victor. To prepare for unfavorable eventualities, citizens of both sides hoarded "hard" money. First, gold and then silver coins were hoarded. Soon even copper-nickel Indian cents were no longer seen in circulation. The effects on commerce were frightening. One could obtain all the $1, $5, or other bills one wanted, but when it came to making small change at the general store for flour, candy, or whatever, there were no coins to be had. The Act of July 17, 1862 authorized a remedy, and over the next few years small paper notes, called fractional currency today, were issued in the denominations of 3, 5, 10, 15, 25, and 50 cents. These were called "stamps" by many citizens, for the earliest issues included representations of current postage stamps as part of their printed design. In the same year, 1862, small cent-size tokens began to appear in circulation, but it was not until the following year that this tide turned to a flood. In 1863 literally thousands of different token varieties were issued by merchants, political interests, and others.

Sometime around the beginning of paper fractional currency issues a privately made and somewhat related product appeared; the encased postage stamp. J. Gault, associated with the firm of Kirkpatrick & Gault, No. 1 Park Place, New York City, patented a unit consisting of several pieces: a front brass frame, a piece of clear mica, an official government United States postage stamp, a thin cardboard filler used as padding, and a back frame. Advertising space embossed on the back frame was sold to various merchants. Stamps of the values of 1, 3, 5, 10, 12, 24, and 90 cents were used, thereby creating encased postage stamps of different denominations.

Many of the mercantile customers were in New York, examples being the Aerated Bread Comany, Lord & Taylor (still very much in business today as a top-line clothing store), Mendum's Family Wine Emporium, and White the Hatter.

Others were more distant. Dr. J.C. Ayer, the patent medicine king headquartered in Lowell, Massachusetts, advertised his Cathartic Pills and his Sarsaparilla, while John Shillito & Co., a Cincinnati department store (still in business today), likewise was a patron. Bailey & Co., the venerable Philadelphia jewelry firm, was an advertiser, as was Joseph L. Bates, a Boston dealer in "Fancy Goods." Even more distant were Weir & Larminie, of Montreal, Canada, and several advertisers in Illinois.

As might be expected, the lower-denomination encased postage stamps were the most popular. Today the valuations of 1, 3, and 5 cents are the most often seen. In general 10-cent issues are scarce, 12-cent pieces are rare, and the higher denominations of 24, 30, and 90 cents are even less often seen. One must be wary when purchasing higher denomination stamps, for some clever (is this the right word?) collectors have learned that what a manufacturing company can put together, a patient craftsman can tear asunder. Accordingly, certain low-value encased postage stamps have been disassembled, and the inexpensive stamps have been replaced with those of 24-cent, 30-cent, or 90-cent values. Unusual in numismatics, encased postage stamps are *fabricated* items, in contrast to coins, medals, and tokens which are simply stamped out with one blow of a coining press.

Encased postage stamps have the further distinction of being of interest to both numismatists and philatelists (stamp collectors). Herman Herst, Jr., the well-known stamp dealer, has written that he has made attractive profits over the years by buying encased postage stamps from coin dealers, who seem to price them relatively reasonably, and selling them at higher prices to stamp collectors—who, apparently, do not have ready sources of supply. Actually, there is no such thing as a really *common* encased postage stamp. At the American Numismatic Association convention held in San Diego in August 1983, I looked for specimens and was able to locate only three dealers with a display. Considering that over 300 dealers had bourse tables at the event, encased postage stamps were certainly elusive there! And yet they are not particularly expensive. Those most often seen, those of the lower denominations as mentioned earlier, cost from about $100 on up, depending upon the general appearance, preservation of the mica, and overall grade. One with the mica in shreds or with holes is apt to sell for much less than one with virtually pristine mica. However, as mica is a mineral substance taken from nature, even the most "perfect" pieces are apt to have some striations.

What are or were Drake's Plantation Bitters, the product advertised on the encased postage stamp mentioned at the beginning of the article? Therein lies a tale. A charming book by Gerald Carson, *The Old Country Store,* contains a chapter, "One for a Man, Two for a Horse," its title taken from the prescription seen on the label of a bottle of an old nostrum or remedy. The chapter deals with old-time patent medicines. I quote a few sentences relevant to the present discussion:

"What kind of whiskey are you drinking nowadays, George?," the boys around the store would ask in the '80s when George pointed his cane at invisible piles of rebel dead, and recalled once more how the general had ridden up to him on his white horse at Antietam, shouting: "George! Stop the slaughter. You've killed enough!"

"Never touch it," George would say. "Nothing for me but Plantation Bitters," indicating the shelf. "I'll take a bottle now."

The category of "bitters" comprised bottled liquids which contained a high proportion of alcohol, nearly 100 proof in numerous instances, and which were advertised as "medicines." This was done for several reasons. First, during the Civil War a tax was slapped on alcohol, but bitters, a "medicine," was taxed at a considerably lower rate. Never mind that a particular bitters manufacturer might advertise, for example, that the product contained pure rye whiskey!

Second, in an era in which temperance societies flourished, when the evils of alcohol were preached from the pulpit, and when saloons were havens for the decadent, the taking of medicinal bitters to improve one's health was a right and proper thing to do. During the Civil War the United States government ordered Hostetter's Bitters, a popular brand, by the boxcar load, leading one historian to comment that Pickett's Charge was probably made less painful by the imbibing of Union soldiers beforehand! Perhaps the most ironic advertising of all was done by certain products which proclaimed themselves to be *temperance* bitters, implying that they contained no alcohol. However, often the alcoholic content was much more substantial than one would normally find in a stiff drink!

For grandma, the local minister, or the director of a nearby chapter of the Anti-Saloon League, people who wouldn't touch "hard stuff," bitters provided the ideal tonic. Hostetter's Celebrated Stomach Bitters at one time was 50 proof. The recommended daily dose of six table-spoonsful was about equal to an ounce and a half of straight whiskey. As Carson noted in his book, "Many a good church member of sound temperance principles accumulated an impressive collection of bitters bottles out in the barn, taking his daily dram as a preventive, a tonic, a builder-upper, a diuretic, and as an alterative, without dreaming that the blessed gift of the Vegetable Kingdom, straight from Nature's Own Laboratory, made him feel frisky because it was spiked. If he did, he never mentioned it!"

Concerning the subject of the present article, the same writer went on to note: "Drake's Plantation Bitters, a favorite of the 1860s and '70s, had a cryptogram on the bottle, S.T.1860.X, which was the subject of endless argument and ingenious theorizing along the country store benches. The talking and guessing helped to advertise the bitters."

Explanations of the legend S.T.1860.X were many, with the most popular being that it was an abbreviation for "Started Trade in 1860 with $10." Before proceeding to the "facts" concerning Drake's Plantation Bitters as advertised by the firm that produced the product, I mention the formula for the tasty substance: "Angostura or calisaya bark 4 ounces, chamomile flowers 1 ounce, cardamom bark 2 drams, orange peel 1 ounce, raisins 1 pound, St. Croix rum 2 gallons. Macerate for one month, then press and filter."

The fact that the product consisted nearly entirely of straight rum was neatly disguised by the roundabout description, "Purely a Vegetable Preparation composed simply of well-known Roots, Herbs and Fruits combined with other properties."

Exactly what "plantation" was being referred to, or what a plantation had to do with the product, is a matter of question, for the proprietor, P.H. Drake & Co., was located at Nos. 53, 55, and 57 Park Place,

New York City—an address which, by the way, was not all that distant from Kirkpatrick & Gault, issuer of encased postage stamps located at No. 1 Park Place, but seemingly was distant from the South and other traditional plantation locations!

The product was put up in bottles, usually of a deep amber color, square, and about 10 inches high. The bottle is what collectors of that sort of thing refer to as a *figural,* for it is in the shape of something else, in this instance a log cabin. The printed label continues the theme and shows a mansion with a plantation owner on horseback overseeing a group of slaves. Apparently P.H. Drake and D.S. Barnes, proprietors of the firm, considered themselves to be benefactors to the world, for a catalogue noted that Drake's Plantation Bitters, "secure in the confidence of suffering humanity creates an appetite, cures weakness, dullness, constipation, dyspepsia, sour stomach, diarrhea, general debility, jaundice, etc."

Further benefits were promised by other products offered by the same company. Mexican Mustang Liniment was billed as having been "tested for over 30 years, and is found to be the most reliable remedy for flesh, bone and muscle ailments ever discovered. It is equally adapted to man and animals." In a testimonial Henry S. Libby, of Charlotte, North Carolina, wrote that he "completely cured a trotting mare of bone-splint and spavin by its use," while S.E. Burchard wrote to say that after applying Mexican Mustang Liniment, injuries sustained from a ladder fall were completely healed and, in the process, he saved over $100 in doctor's bills.

Magnolia Water, another P.H. Drake & Co., product, was advertised as an indispensable toilet luxury. "A small quanity of it mingled with a bath has a marked and delightful effect. . . So potent is its influence in allaying the flushed appearance induced by heat and toil, and adding to beauty a new and fresher bloom, that it has frequently been compared to the enchanted waters of the Fountain of Perennial Youth." Hagan's Magnolia Balm apparently was a related product that was issued under the imprint of the Lyon Manufacturing Company, a firm controlled by P.H. Drake & Co. Lyon's Kathairon "for preserving, restoring and beautifying the hair and to prevent its falling off and turning gray" was likewise sold. Sea Moss Farine, said to have been made from Iceland moss or carrageen, was particularly recommmended for pulmonary afflictions. Still another product was Gettysburg Katalysine Water, said to have been bottled on the historic battlefield of Civil War fame but dispensed through P.H. Drake & Co.

But the product of products, the most heavily advertised, remained Drake's Plantation Bitters. To help spread the word the mysterious slogan S.T.1860.X. was plastered everywhere; at Niagara Falls, where thousands of tourists could not help but notice it, along the main line of the Pennsylvania Railroad, and on numerous posters and billboards. It was reported that an effort was made to emblazon the slogan on the side of the Great Pyramid in Egypt but that Drake's offer was declined! In 1871, in the almanac *Morning, Noon and Night,* an explanation was given:

"S.T.1860.X., like the initials on the old Roman banners, has a meaning. It represents St. Croix—S.T. being the conventional equivalent of Saint and 1-8-6-0 standing for the letters C-R-O-I, and so forming, with the concluding X, the word CROIX. Nothing can be more simple, or, it may be, more appropriate. St. Croix rum is a stimulating basis of the Plantation Bitters, and it is, therefore, in accordance with the fitness of things, that St. Croix should be the basis of their business shibboleth."

In what surely must be a case of early-day *chutzpah,* the same almanac recommended Plantation Bitters as a cure for hangovers! Read on:

Plantation Bitters as a morning tonic. Nausea, physical exhaustion, a confused brain, trembling hands, and a general incapacity for business are the usual morning consequences of undue indulgence in any intoxicating beverage the night before. The morning difficulty is met by those who are foolish enough to incur it, in various ways. In one case the victim drenches his already weakened stomach with soda water; in another, takes the drastic purgative; in a third tries "a hair of the dog that bit him," and endeavors to set himself up with a morning dram. All these attempts to restore the system to a normal condition are injudicious—the last worst of all. . . . It is obvious, therefore, that a stomachic, a nervine, an antibillious medicine, a mild aperient, and a harmless exhilarant are the remedies indicated. PLANTATION BITTERS comprises all these elements, and is consequently the specific required. It invariably relieves all the unpleasant symptoms, and if a small dose of it is taken before breakfast, and another about 10 or 11 o'clock, the effect of the previous night's dissipation will have disappeared by the hour of noon. It would be the height of folly, however, to indulge in inebriety because this fine vegetable tonic is the best means of arresting its secondary results, inasmuch as hard drinking tells, sooner or later, upon the constitution itself, an exhaustive vital system. It would be about as wise to permit the wheels of a delicate machine to become unnecessarily clogged with dust and filth, because a brush and sweet oil will cleanse them, as to indulge in habitual intoxications, because PLANTATION BITTERS will cure the disagreeable sensations occasioned by casual intemperance.

Not to worry. At the recommended dosage of three wineglassfuls a day, it seems that "the previous night's dissipation" would just blend into the inebriety of the following evening!

Apparently the motto S.T.1860.X., notwithstanding the previously printed explanation, derives part of its form from 1860, the year in which the concoction was first sold. Almost from the point of inception, the product caught on like wildfire. A few years later the firm was to boast:

> The popularity of Plantation Bitters is founded on a rock of experience. Its name is as familiar to every household in the land as that of the ordinary staples of life, and it ranks as an article of prime necessity wherever sickness is present or health is in peril.
>
> The continual increase in the consumption of Plantation Bitters—to which, judging from present indications, there is no assignable limit—demands from year to year a corresponding increase in the facilities of its manufacturer. In 1868 the sales were nearly 5 million bottles, and the sales for 1869 are already upwards of 6¼ millions. To keep pace with a growing demand, large and costly additions have been made by Drake & Co. to the machinery, etc., in their manufactory, and many ingenious improvements have been introduced in the chemical department which greatly expedite the production of the article. New inventions have also been applied in the bottling and packing departments, by which the repetity of these processes has been promoted, and several new receivers of extraordinary capacity have been added to the ranges of tanks previously in use. The factory is now capable of turning out nearly 10 million bottles annually, and at the present rate of increase in the demand, that quantity will be barely sufficient to fill the orders, foreign and domestic, for 1875.
>
> The business has attained its present vast proportions in the short period of nine years [this was written in 1869—Ed.]—a specimen of commercial progress which it would be difficult to match in the mercantile history of even this go-ahead country. It would

be an insult to the proverbial sagacity of the people to ask if any save an *article of sterling value* could have obtained the commanding position now occupied by the Plantation Bitters in the national market. . . Only a few mercantile establishments in this country yield a clear income larger than the amount annually expanded in the *mere advertising* of the Plantation Bitters, to say nothing of the cost of materials and manufacture, the charges for transportation, the duties paid to the government, and other incidental expenses. When it is remembered that the ability to afford these immense disbursements is founded solely on the pecuniary success of the article, and that it is only nine years since it was first offered to the world, the public can guess for themselves what that success must have been. They will see, too, that it cannot be based on anything but the *superior merits of the preparation* that has achieved this unprecedented triumph.

In 1870 the firm was to proclaim that its almanac, *Morning, Noon and Night,* was distributed yearly to the extent of 6 million copies at a cost of $120,000. Success went to the heads of those in charge, and soon fortune-telling was engaged in. Obviously, those writing advertising copy at Drake & Co., considered themselves to be oracles on just about every area of life imaginable. Comments on the morality of individuals in New York and Paris society were printed, as were observations about Englishmen, the summer season at Saratoga Springs (New York), and the activities of pawnbrokers. Predictions for the future were printed with reckless abandon. With a shotgun approach, it was inevitable that some of these would bear fruit. Disregarding numerous failed predictions, the advertising copy noted in 1871 of the success of the forecasts of the previous year, 1870:

The singularly accurate fulfillment of some of the prophecies for 1870, made in the last issue of *Morning, Noon and Night,* occasioned no small amount of astonishment among its multitudinous readers. Letters have been received from professors of astrology in various parts of the country inquiring the character of the celestial indicia upon which the predictions were based, the method of calculation employed in arriving at conclusions so truthful. Other parties, who seemed to have mistaken our scientific contributor for an ordinary soothsayer, have written for information as to their future, in pretty much the same style as if they had been addressing some advertising charlatan, who retails his blind guesses at so much per fib. Once and for all, we would say that the gentleman who furnishes the annual horoscope, and other astrological data for this publication, limits his prophecy to its pages. He has faith in astrology, of which he has unquestionably a more profound knowledge than any other man on this side of the Atlantic. . .

In those days of long ago it was the custom for many, if not most, newspapers to accept patent medicine advertising on a contract basis, often guaranteeing that favorable editorial material would appear in conjunction with the paid for space. Thus, newspaper articles such as this one from the *New York Tribune* must be taken, as they say, with a grain of salt:

> Calisaya Bark. It is said that P.H. Drake & Co., proprietors of the Plantation Bitters, are the largest importers of calisaya bark in this country, and that with the exception of an occasional sale, that all they import is used in the compounding of the celebrated Plantation Bitters, and to which they are undoubtedly indebted for their wonderful health restoring properties; as a tonic and appetizer they are not surpassed, and we can cheerfully recommend them.

In the 1860s and 1870s, as now, the earth would have been depopulated if everyone contracting an upset stomach, a restless feeling, aches and pains, and other maladies were to end up in a funeral parlor a few days later. Unattended, most such distresses take care of themselves. Thus, tormented souls who took Drake's Plantation Bitters had no better odds of recovery, for or against, than people who had never heard of the substance. But, considering the nearly complete alcoholic content of The Product, perhaps imbibers of Plantation Bitters *enjoyed* their illness more!

As might be expected, the enthusiastic, aggressive, and widespread advertising of Drake's Plantation Bitters spawned a number of competitors. What owner of a chemical or patent medicine firm would not be jealous when reading of the annual production figures of millions of bottles? So, numerous imitations arose. There were, for example, O.K. Plantation Bitters and Woodgate's Plantation Bitters, each put up in a log cabin format amber bottle measuring 10 inches high and looking for all the world just like the Drake's product. Perhaps the most intriguing imitator of all was E. Dexter Loveridge, who made the enchantingly named Wahoo Bitters, complete with his own imitation of S.T.1860.X, a cryptogram which read: D.W.D.1863.X.X.X.! The exclamation point, we might clarify, is ours, not that of Mr. Loveridge's advertising writer.

Wahoo Bitters differed somewhat in composition in that instead of St. Croix rum it contained another equally efficacious product, to wit:

The Wahoo Bitters are entirely vegetable, being composed of some 20 different roots and barks. This compound was procured in part from the most eminent Indian physicians known among our northwestern tribes; the balance from my own botanical research, and is a profound secret, making the best compound ever invented for the preservation of health. The spirits used to preserve these bitters so that they will keep in any climate is not an adulterated alcohol, flavored with poisonous drugs, and claimed to be a foreign importation, but is PURE RYE WHISKEY. . .

Drake's Plantation Bitters had its heyday in the 1860s and early 1870s, but apparently the product was marketed for at least a decade or two after that, for mention of it crops up in an 1889 report.

Other bitters manufacturers ignored the log cabin and plantation theme and went in other directions. The naming of The Product became an art, and the more obscure or confusing the name, the better! Thus such products as Dr. Hardy's Cathartic Electuary Bitters, Carey's Grecian Bend Bitters, Schroeder's Woodcock Pepsin Bitters, Tincture of Centaury Bitters, Exculapea Bitters, Dr. Doty's Celebrated Mandrake Freedom and Unity Bitters, Barto's Great Gun Bitters, and the immodestly named Best Bitters in America each attracted a following. Typically, labels proclaimed a generous alcohol content, then carefully noted that the substance was present only as a preservative!

Today Drake's Plantation Bitters is a product long since forgotten, except, perhaps, to numismatists and others interested in encased postage stamps, and to bottle collectors.

From Rare Coin Review *No. 50, January-March 1984.*

The Coin Outlasts the Throne

| By Frank Morton Todd | 1970 |

*T*his article was written by Mr. Todd and published in 1921 in Volume IV of The Story of the Exposition. Farran Zerbe's numismatic accomplishments were many, and included the presidency of the American Numismatic Association, the adoption of the 1921 Peace design silver dollar, and the formation of an extensive collection of coins—a collection which later formed the basis of the Chase Manhattan Bank Money Museum exhibit. This 1921 article presents a contemporary view of one of the most colorful individuals in American numismatics.

Farran Zerbe was once a newsboy in Tyrone, Pennsylvania. He had a bank account. He was very proud of it, and proud also of the accuracy with which he made out his deposit slips and conducted his other small transactions. One day he took in change a queer piece of money. It was a silver coin about the size of a dime, and it bore odd, misspelled words, which to the gimlet-eyed newsboy meant nothing. There was upon it, however, the legend "50 cent." So it was a half dollar, although a bit stunted in its growth, and he counted it for a half dollar and tried to deposit it for a half dollar.

But the cashier said, "What are you trying on us, Farran? You're 50 cents short. And you've got a piece of French money here. That's no good in this country."

Farran Zerbe was a numismatist, but he didn't know it yet—and wouldn't have known the difference between a numismatist and a counterfeiter. That was the first time it had come to his attention that there were more kinds of money than Uncle Sam made, and he was a bit incredulous. If there had been any other kinds of importance, people would have known about them and they would have circulated on the streets of Tyrone, Pennsylvania; but he had never heard of any. Yet there was this troublesome dime, marked "50 cent," when it wasn't. He had an itching curiosity to know how it had come about.

He began to ask questions. The cashier was glad to answer them. Then Zerbe began to read everything he could get hold of about coins and medals and the strange things people had used in primitive stages of civilization as a medium of exchange. He got acquainted with those people, ancient and modern. Being a numismatist involved a great deal he had never contemplated. It was worse, really, than being a philatelist! It led him into strange fields. He could never read Old Sleuth like the other boys; he was sleuthing through translated Hesiod, trying to find out what the ancient Greeks used for money, and why they did.

Being a numismatist he became a geographer, an anthropologist, an archeologist, an historian, an economist, a student of governments, and political systems, and religions, and mythology, and symbolism, and heraldry, and art. He collected coins, currency, medals. He corresponded with scholars and societies of scholars. He became president of the American Numismatic Association, a member of the U.S. Assay Commission, and publisher of *The Numismatist*.

For Farran Zerbe, the 50-centime piece was the gateway into a broad and liberal intellectual life, a life of absorbing, unending interest; and money in general became, not riches, nor especially a thing to buy luxuries or liquidate debts, nor yet a thing to propagate, but a documentary record of the progress of man and the stages of his civilization at different epochs. Coins were imperishable metal documents, and types of art indicative of the refinement and mental energy of the nations producing them. The money of civilized peoples became a chain reaching back, unbroken, 3,000 years, correcting history and contributing to it, and reaching back with some breaks and interruptions not yet linked up, for 2,000 years more.

Zerbe never cared to acquire a coin or a medal for its rarity, but only for what it could tell. In spite of that limitation his collection grew very large. Because of that limitation it became one of the notable collections of the world. He could tell you things about coins and medals you never thought of before; trifling things that might become clues to the lost episodes in the lives of nations, economically fundamental things about the essential nature of a medium of exchange from the plough beasts of Ulysses to California "slugs." He knew the mintmarks and the marks of the great coin designers. He knew the delight the scholar derives from getting hold of a contemporary portrait of Caesar or of Alexander, passed by the sitter and stamped by the government, and how, when such a portrait is a good piece of art, it authenticates the genius of a people who could breed artists capable of such work.

He added some notable borrowings to his collection and brought them all to the Panama-Pacific International Exposition in San Francisco in 1915. The exhibit was installed in the Palace of Liberal Arts, in which department it belonged under the classification, making as a whole the greatest index to money ever collectively displayed, and the most noteworthy numismatic exhibit ever seen at an American exposition.

There were about 20,000 original specimens of what man at the main stages of his evolution and in all known countries has used as money, and the whole collection represented a one-time value of at least $50 million.

There were clay tablets of accounts from Nippur, constituting a record of values measured in labor, love, stock, and grain. There were implement-shaped metal pieces from China, meant to be the fixed price of the article represented, for even in ancient times people befuddled themselves with the supposition that government could fix prices permanently—a knife-shaped coin, for example, standing for the price of a knife. There were "plugs" of brick tea, stamped by the Russian government, notched so they could be broken into small change, and circulated among the peoples of Tibet; long black strips of licorice-soaked tobacco, pierced so they could be strung for necklaces, made in Petersburg, Virginia, and circulated as money in certain South Pacific islands, where they would buy more than anything else you could take there; a slab of copper two feet long, a foot wide, and an inch or so thick, which was once eight dollars in Sweden; and gold coins of some Indian state that were no larger than a pinhead. There was leather money, paper money, shells, wampum of all descriptions, rubber money, condensed milk money, bone, fiber, clay, coal, glass, cloth, and pasteboard, and there were linen notes, and iron coins in the shape of fish hooks and musket balls. There were Russian platinum coins minted when platinum was so little valued it was thought only good to make jitneys with. There was every kind of wildcat note, including the money of John Law and his Mississippi Bubble. There were interesting historical and financial documents—checks of many presidents, from Washington to Lincoln. There was a check for half a cent, and a photograph of the government voucher for $40 million in payment for the French interests in the Panama Canal. There were notes redeemable in rum. And there were private coinages such as the 50-dollar slugs of California, beaver coins of Oregon, Mormon issues of Utah, and the Bechtler coins of the South.

There were coins here that showed something about the art, architecture, mythology, religion, sports, and pleasures of every period of Greece in her glory, and Rome in her fall. The deterioration that followed the universal tragedy of a dead empire was reflected in the barbarous crudities of the coins of the Dark Ages. There was siege money in all its variety; the devices of besieged cities to carry on business in spite of war. It told sometimes of lost causes, of nations going down; it suggested civilizations destroyed and forgotten.

The collection aroused great interest in the subject of numismatics, and well it might. It was one of the most definite educational factors of the Exposition.

The Exposition Coins and Medals

On the basis of the Federal legislation the Exposition instituted an official Coin and Medal Department, and put it under the direction of Farran Zerbe. The Act of Congress provided that a series of commemorative medals; a souvenir medal, the award medal, and the diplomas, were to be produced by the government and delivered to the Exposition at face value for the coins and at cost for the other items. The secretary of the Treasury was authorized to obtain suitable designs; but the Exposition had no voice in the selection of them, and did not know what the coins would look like until they were finally delivered.

Owing to the lateness of the date on which the Act of Congress was passed—January 16, 1915—it was impossible to have any of the coins produced until about three months after the opening of the Exposition. In order to have them then, dies for the gold dollar were made by a private concern at the Exposition's expense, and they were probably the first United States coin dies to be made by other than government employees since the practical organization of the Mint.

In spite of the delay, the Coinage Department took in $179,506 in the Exposition period, and $51,966 in the post-Exposition period. The whole net return of the Exposition's coin and medal business after deducting the cost of materials and all administration expenses came to $65,555.09.

60,000 commemorative half dollars were coined, of which 34 were reserved for assay. Of the 59,966 pieces available, 27,100 were sold and 32,866 were destroyed later at the Mint. 25,034 gold dollars were coined, of which 34 were used for assay and the balance all sold. 10,017 $2½ gold pieces were struck of which 17 were used for assay, leaving 10,000 available. Of these 10,000 there were 6,750 sold and the rest, 3,250 pieces, were melted.

There were 1,509 of the octagonal $50 gold pieces made of which nine were used for assay. 646 were actually sold and 854 went to the melting pot. There were 1,510 round $50 gold pieces including 10 for assay. Just 483 were sold. 1,017 were melted.

All of the commemorative Exposition coins were struck at the San Francisco Mint and bear the "S" mintmark. For the coining of the $50 pieces a special hydraulic press weighing 14 tons, with a striking power of 450 tons, ordinarily used at the Philadelphia Mint for striking medals, was delivered to the San Francisco Mint.

The striking of the first octagonal $50 gold piece, the largest coin ever authorized by the government, and the first of any other shape than circular, was made a notable occasion at the Mint, as the passage of an act authorizing it was a rare tribute to California and the Exposition. The superintendent, Mr. T.W.H. Shanahan, extended invitations to various dignitaries and to members of the American Numismatic Association, to be present at 11:00 on the morning of June 21, 1915 when the first of these coins was struck.

Superintendent Shanahan produced the first piece, saying that he was about to strike the first $50 coin ever issued under authority of law in the United States. He then pulled the lever and handed the resultant coin to Mr. Moore for inspection. Moore then operated the lever for the second piece, and other members of the party took their turns at making money, keeping up the delightful exercise until lunch time.

The various commemorative coins were in good demand. Advance orders amounted to a sales value of $40,000. Prices were: half dollars, $1 each or six for $5. Gold dollars, $2 each, or six for $10. $2½ gold pieces, $4 each or six for $20. $50 gold pieces, either shape, $100 each. Complete sets mounted in metal frames or leather cases sold for $200. That both shapes of the $50 pieces were of the same design was a disappointment and in many cases limited the sale to one coin. On this account, towards the close of the Exposition, sets with a choice of one $50 piece were sold at $100 each.

Many sales were made to banks throughout the country. Usually these were of sets mounted in metal (copper) frames. With the close of the Exposition this exhibit was moved to the Palace of Fine Arts where it looked very much at home and continued as a sales agency for the Exposition over the post-Exposition period to May 1, 1916. The Coin and Medal Department was continued on a mail order basis down to November 1, 1916 when, at the request of the Exposition and by authority of the secretary of the Treasury, the coins remaining unsold were returned to the Mint and destroyed.

From Rare Coin Review *No. 5, May 1970.*

A Visit With B. Max Mehl

By Q. David Bowers | 1983

Unquestionably, B. Max Mehl, of Fort Worth, Texas, was America's most colorful dealer during the early part of the present century. Born in Lithuania in 1884, Mehl came to America at an early age. As a teenager he became a clerk in a shoe store, perhaps intending to make this his life's business. But an interest in numismatics intervened, as did a flair for advertising and public relations.

In December 1903 a half-page advertisement appeared in *The Numismatist*. Thirty-three different lots of coins and paper money, some of which probably had been recently culled from circulation (such as worn examples of the 1892 and 1893 Columbian half dollars), were offered to the highest bidders. This advertisement set the stage for many to come. By July 1906 Mehl was able to announce: "With pleasure I beg to advise my friends and patrons that I now devote all my time to the coin business. Before it was only a 'sideline' with me, but thanks to the esteemed patronage favored me by many of the faithful, my business grew to such an extent that I was obliged to abandon all other interests and devote all my time in serving those who find me worthy of a share of their esteemed numismatic favors. . ." Presumably, Fort Worth citizens desiring properly fitted shoes had to look elsewhere after this time.

It wasn't long before Mehl was issuing his own monthly magazine, attending American Numismatic Association conventions with regularity, and conducting mail bid "auctions." Many fine collections started coming his way, including the James Ten Eyck holdings in 1922, one of the finest American coin cabinets ever dispersed.

In 1931 Mehl announced that he had spent $18,500 for a single advertisement to sell his coin book, *The Star Rare Coin Encyclopedia and Premium Catalogue,* to readers of the *American Weekly* Sunday magazine. The editor of *The Numismatist,* recognizing Mehl's "spreading of the gospel" across America, said in print, "Again we congratulate you, Max."

Mehl did not stop with the printed word. At one time his radio program was beamed to countless listeners. Other numismatists were equally enthusiastic about the new broadcast medium, and Moritz Wormser, president of the American Numismatic Association and, later (beginning in 1936), proprietor of the New Netherlands Coin Company, also took to the airwaves, as did several other collectors and dealers.

The present writer first met B. Max Mehl at a convention in 1955, two years before his death. We had a nice conversation, with Abe Kosoff providing the introduction. In 1957, following Mehl's death, Kosoff handled many items from his estate. Interestingly, the name and trademark effects of Mehl were offered for sale for $25,000. Numerous potential buyers, including the present writer, were contacted, but apparently few could see changing the name of their business to the B. Max Mehl Company. Finally a buyer was found: George Justus, of Beverly Hills, California, who conducted an enterprise under that name for a number of years thereafter.

Browsing through an old bookstore in Wells, Maine recently, I subsequently emerged with a pasteboard carton full of books. Almost as an afterthought a copy of *The Star Rare Coin Encyclopedia and Premium Catalogue,* 1930 edition, was added to the pile. I had seen editions of the book many times earlier and, years ago, virtually every numismatic library acquired in conjunction with a collection possessed one or more copies. Now, however, such publications are becoming scarce. I put the Mehl publication with a pile of clippings, correspondence, and other things, intending to file it. Then an idle moment arose, and I decided to read some of the words that Mehl had written many years ago. I had quite forgotten what the *Encyclopedia* contained. It turned out that far from being a premium list, the book or booklet (take your pick; it is 206 pages in length, plus covers) was a veritable gold mine of solid numismatic information. While I am sure that the main intended purpose was to make a nice profit by selling these to the public at a dollar each, with a secondary benefit of acquiring rare coins inexpensively, another benefit had to be the creation of new collectors for the hobby. Indeed, it was precisely this direction which prompted the

American Numismatic Association to give Max its congratulations.

How many of these publications were issued? Probably *millions.* At one time the Fort Worth Post Office related that over 70% of its business concerned B. Max Mehl's activities! Mehl kept dozens of workers busy opening sacks of mail, plucking out coins and paper money, and mailing catalogues. Mehl's offer to pay $50 for a 1913 Liberty Head nickel received nationwide attention, with the result that a leading metropolitan trolley car company complained that its business was being impaired by conductors who slowed up the pace of things by carefully examining every nickel before putting it in the register box! Alas, no prize 1913 Liberty Head nickels were ever found in circulation by any readers of *The Star Rare Coin Encyclopedia and Premium Catalogue,* but it was not for the want of looking!

Today, one can have an interesting "visit" with B. Max Mehl simply by looking at the *Catalogue* from cover to cover.

To begin with, the cover is decorated by four coins, each of numismatic significance. On the left is an 1850 Baldwin $10 gold piece of the "Horseman" type. In the center, obverse and reverse, is shown what probably is intended to be an 1804 silver dollar, but which is reproduced half dollar-size. There is no such thing as an 1804 half dollar (although the 1805/4 overdate comes close), so without question the dollar was intended. To the right, illustrating the cosmopolitan aspect of the *Encyclopedia,* is shown a British coin of Oliver Cromwell.

At the bottom of the cover appears an engraving of the three-story Mehl Building. In keeping with stock certificates, factory advertisements, and other printed material issued by successful merchants of the time, the up-to-date aspect of Mehl's business was pointed up by a trolley car, that most modern of conveniences, and a four-door roadster (the latter parked at the front entrance). Appearing like something one might find in the French Quarter of New Orleans, the building, identified with the large word "MEHL" at the top front, center, was decorated with several balconies with ornate railings. The print at the bottom noted that B. Max Mehl was the owner and manager of The Numismatic Company of Texas, Unincorporated, which was formerly known as The Numismatic Bank.

Turning the page one, encounters a notice, "PLEASE READ THIS BEFORE WRITING OR SENDING US COINS." Apparently Mehl was troubled by people who acquired the *Encyclopedia,* who didn't read it, but who rushed to send him all sorts of worthless pieces, leaving it up to Mehl to send his check for a generous amount. "The prices quoted in this book are those we pay for the coins. If you want to *buy* coins, send 10 cents for our large illustrated selling list, showing our selling prices for coins and bills." No sirree, $125 was the *buying* price for an 1875 $3 piece, not what numismatically sharp B. Max Mehl would sell one for! The notice at the front of the *Encyclopedia* reads:

> The prices quoted are those we PAY, and depend entirely upon the condition of the coins. If a half dollar is quoted at 50 cents, it indicates that it is worth only face value. The dates of United States coins not given in this book are not worth any premiums. It is therefore a waste of time for anyone to write for special quotations, etc. All questions as to conditions, prices, etc., are answered in this book. By reading pages four to seven carefully before writing us or sending us coins, much trouble and useless correspondence will be avoided. When you write, be sure to enclose a self-addressed stamped envelope to insure reply. Our mail is so large that the postage on replies would amount to a considerable sum, while the cost to you is but two cents.

As anyone in the mail-order business knows, a certain percentage of customers are quick to fire shotgun blasts at any advertiser who does not perform quickly at the snap of a finger. Let a week go by without a reply or delivery of the merchandise, and the mail-order advertiser is a crook, or worse! Mehl realized this, and on the inside front cover he noted:

> We fill orders the same day as received, but please remember there are three links to a mail order transaction—yourself, ourselves, and the United States mail. If any link is defective, an error occurs; letters and third class mail at times go astray, and at times we receive remittances without name and address. Despite all care on our side, errors will occur. If delay or non-delivery occurs, please seek a direct explanation before jumping to any conclusion. . . .

This prompts the present writer to recollect a situation which happened about 15 years ago. A prospective client sent several dollars in cash ordering a numismatic book. The only trouble was that no name or address was included. The order was set aside in a folder reserved for such things (this situation was and is not uncommon). A few weeks went by, and then came a threatening letter. "Unless I receive the book by return mail, I will notify the postal authorities!" You guessed it: no name or address on that letter either! A few weeks later we were given another chance before the wrath of the United States government was called down on our head. Still no name or address given! Finally we received a telephone call, collect, from a very irate man who told us in no uncertain terms that what we were doing was illegal—keeping his money and not sending him a book. The cost of the telephone call wiped out any profit on the small transaction, but at least we were able to find out who and where he was, so all was settled peaceably.

The title page of *The Star Rare Coin Encyclopedia and Premium Catalogue* advised the reader that at hand was the 34th edition "containing large lists of ancient, medieval and modern coins of the world from 500 BC down to the present time, about 2,000 illustrations, the most complete and authentic work of its kind published."

Further, the title page went on to say that it contained: "complete lists of all rare United States and colonial coins, private and territorial gold, United States fractional currency, Confederate and colonial notes, encased postage stamps, rare Canadian coins, and a complete list of standard foreign coins and notes and their approximate value in United States money, together with valuable and authentic information and specially-prepared articles on coins and coinage, showing prices paid for same."

Back in 1981 when I was writing a series of columns, "How to Be a Successful Coin Dealer," for the weekly publication *Coin World* (actually an update of a booklet I had written 10 years earlier), I scanned dealers' advertisements and found no fewer than four firms claiming to be "the largest dealer in the world" or "the largest dealer in the United States," although one dealer modestly claimed to be "the largest dealer in the East" (leaving the presumption that a larger dealer was located somewhere in the West). In 1930 Mehl proclaimed on his title page that he was the "largest rare coin establishment in the United States." In that year, he had few competitors. Probably no one disputed the statement.

Page three was illustrated and showed the Saint-Gaudens $10 and $20 issues of 1907 together with an ancient Greek coin with a flying eagle and an ancient silver coin of Egypt with a standing eagle, showing that nothing was new under the numismatic sun. "The more things change, the more they stay the same," someone once said.

Then came some general information concerning coins. "Never clean a rare coin," Mehl wrote. "A somewhat corroded coin is oftentimes more valuable than a cleaned one. The cleaning of a rare coin considerably decreases its value."

Lest some reader possessed with a worthless coin question the writer's credentials, it was noted: "The prices offered in this book are not of mere guesswork. This book was prepared with the greatest care as to accuracy, after years of close study of the values of rare coins, with the assistance of years of experience gained in the coin business."

A few paragraphs later came a discussion of grading, followed by definitions of such terms as "restrikes," "altered dates," "electrotypes," "cast coins," and "forgeries."

After that point began a listing of United States issues together with values. A 1793 half cent commanded a price of $1 to $5, Proof half cents of the 1840s were worth $5 to $20 to Mehl, the popular 1856 Flying Eagle cent was valued at $3 to $5, and the elusive 1877 of the same denomination brought five cents to 25 cents. It is to be remembered that in 1930 the *retail* prices of coins were but the merest fractions of later values, and the offering of 25 cents for an 1877 Indian cent might represent the purchase of a coin which would retail for a little more than a dollar or two. Mehl did not skimp on photographs, and just about every other page of the book was devoted to pictures. Interestingly, the pictures in general were not all coordinated with the text. For example, facing descriptions of nickel five-cent pieces were illustrations of various United States silver dollars, while $10 gold coins illustrated the section on early dimes. It obviously was the intent of Mehl to create a handsome volume which would be much admired, not to provide a text with illustrations that could be closely followed in logical order from beginning to end. Only the most erudite of numismatists would have been able to understand Plate 22, which, by the way, faced an introduction to California gold coins, which showed the 1792 half disme, the rare ROSA SINE SPINA Rosa Americana pattern, and other esoteric issues!

In the realm of esoterica or, as we say in modern times, trivia, was a listing of "failed Canadian banks and banks in liquidation whose bills are worthless." Hence we learn that the Bank of Western Canada in Clifton, Ontario issued valueless paper as did Zimmerman's Bank, Elgin, Ontario. Probably not one *Encyclopedia* buyer in a million would have desired this information!

The more one reads this attractive little book, the more one realizes the volume would have been more useful to numismatists than to the general public. For example, page 112 listed in detail the weight and fineness of various United States coin denominations, followed by tests to determine whether gold and silver bullion was good or bad. And, it would have taken an enthusiastic numismatist to have appreciated the article on the pattern $50 gold pieces of 1877 which appeared from page 179 through 183. Likewise, the two-page article on encased postage stamps, the article "The Petition Crown of Thomas Simon," and "The Glass Coins of China" were in the realm of the serious collector. With the exception of the coin prices, which are woefully out of date, *The Star Rare Coin Encyclopedia* is a book which could be handed today to a beginning collector to inspire him toward greater numismatic achievements! As such, the worth of the *Encyclopedia* has been long overlooked, in the present writer's opinion. Perhaps here is a candidate for reprinting by some modern day publisher!

The Texas dealer wrapped up his 206-page book with numerous coins for sale. A type set of 22 different United States coins from the cent to the dollar was available for $14.25, or a half cent could be obtained for 35 cents, a Flying Eagle cent for a dime, or a 20-cent piece could be bought for 75 cents. Twenty-five different broken bank notes could be had for $8.50, while 15 different fractional currency issues cost $10.50. A set of California gold pieces comprising two quarter dollars and two half dollars could be ordered for $3. To help spread the word about coin collecting, the inside back cover of the book gave Mehl's philosophy on the subject:

COLLECT COINS for Pleasure and Profit. Coin collecting as a hobby affords more pleasure and greater interest than any other collectable objects. It opens a wide field of study. It develops a taste for art and stimulates research in nearly every branch of learning. It teaches us history and geography, and while a very fascinating and instructive pastime, it has also been the source of much profit, as no one knows better than those who have collected coins in the past, that coin collections increase in value from year to year, thus providing an excellent investment. Coins are often the only historical records that we have of nations which have long since passed away, and which would have been buried in oblivion but for the coins that bear the names of kings and records and events relating to the countries whose money they once were.

From Rare Coin Review *No. 49, October-December 1983.*

The Wonderful World of Large Cents

By *Denis Loring*   *1972*

I love large cents. In the words of Dr. William Sheldon, "They are an intriguing family, and they never die, fade, or get broken. Like good jewelry they seem to transcend human mortality and to grow richer with age. . . The early cents carry the memory, and an indelible impression, of a little stretch of human time that was fragrant with a high hope." They also form one of the most fascinating of all series of United States coins, a series replete with strange and unusual varieties. You'll see what I mean in just a moment, but first let's look at the big pennies in general.

Mr. Average Collector will probably first encounter large cents as part of a type collection. He'll need seven coins, of which two (both 1793, the first year of issue) are expensive. If the large cent bug bites, he may start a date collection of the big coppers. This will require 64 pieces, one each from 1793 through 1857, with the exception of 1815. Only three of these years 1793, 1799, and 1804 will run into a little money. The next step might be a date and major variety collection, perhaps using the *Guide Book of United States Coins*. Not counting the two varieties listed as "extremely rare," our collecting friend will now be after 145 coins to complete his set. But now a mere bankroll will not be enough, especially if he wants choice coins. He'll have to do some hard-nosed hunting, and patience is most definitely a virtue. (To the skeptic, I suggest the following: call up your fraction dealer and ask him when he last had an 1803 Large Date, Small Fraction cent in stock—and how long he kept it!)

Variety collecting is the final step in the progression of the large cent disease. *Variety* here means *die variety*; each combination of obverse and reverse dies is considered a different variety and collectible entity. Usually, subvarieties (same dies but different edge devices) are collected as well. This variety game is a formidable one indeed; one year alone, 1794, offers no fewer than 66 varieties (and subvarieties), of which four are unique! Two reference books serve as bibles for variety collectors, *Penny Whimsy* by Dr. William H. Sheldon, Dorothy I. Paschal, and Walter Breen, deals with the years 1793-1814, called the early dates. There are now 345 varieties of early dates known; the most recent discovery was only months ago. Howard R. Newcomb's book, *United States Copper Cents 1816-1857,* covers the rest of the series, the late dates. Of these, many collectors are interested in only the 1816-1835 series (the "Tammany Heads") of which 182 varieties are currently known, others run right through 1857. Some large cent buffs specialize in specific years (1794, for example) or types (such as the Draped Bust, 1796-1807), others collect the entire early series, or the late dates, or both. In fact, there are a few enthusiasts who collect by die *state* trying to trace the various die break progressions of each die variety!

With this introduction, let's take a look at some of the weird and wonderful denizens of the world of large cents.

The very first large cent, Sheldon number one (S-1), is the 1793 Chain AMERI, pronounced "AM-er-eye." The engraver, probably Jean-Pierre Droz, was afraid that he had not left enough room for the entire word AMERICA, and so abbreviated it to AMERI. This error was not repeated when the next reverse die was cut, and the several Chain AMERICA varieties resulted.

1793 is also the year of the famous Strawberry Leaf cents. These cents, of the same general design as other 1793 Wreath cents, are distinguished by the sprig of strawberry (or perhaps cotton or clover) leaves, instead of the usual olive leaves, above the date. The origin of these notorious cents is not definitely known. Some claim they are a legitimate Mint product, others view them as pattern or experimental pieces, while still others classify them as contemporary counterfeits. Exactly four Strawberry Leaf cents are known to exist; three share one reverse die, while the fourth is unique. Periodically, rumors of another specimen circulate, but to date all searches have been fruitless.

Moving on to 1794, we enounter one of the most famous and highly prized of all the large cents: the Starred Reverse, S-48. This variety features a circle of 94 tiny, five-pointed stars around the extreme outer edge of the reverse. The stars are not quite evenly spaced, though extremely well formed, and they are partially obscured by the denticles. The variety is considered by Don Taxay (from his *Scott's Encyclopedia of United States Coins*) to be a Philadelphia Mint essay, while Sheldon feels ". . .it is perhaps more likely that they [the stars] are the result of the whim of an idle hour at the Mint." Approximately 30 specimens of the Starred Reverse are known to exist.

There is perhaps no better indicator of the recent upsurge of interest in large cents than in the auction records of the Starred Reverse over the past decade. In 1961, The Schwartz coin, almost Very Good, brought $115. In early 1969 a Fine specimen sold for $400. This past May, the Central States Convention auction featured the Frank Masters collection of large cents. Included was a Starred Reverse, offered as Fine. After a furious floor fight, the coin was knocked down for $1,600—and resold for a profit the next day!

The year 1795 is responsible for two unusual cents. One is the excessively rare Reeded Edge variety, S-79. This coin was a short-lived experiment on the part of the Mint, which was in the process of changing from lettered-edge to plain-edge planchets. Six specimens are known, of which one is a brockage. The other 1795 celebrity is the famous Jefferson Head cent. The Jeffersons are quite distinctive in appearance. The head of Liberty is different from that on any other cent, and, with the aid of a little imagination, the profile does seem to resemble that of our third president. The reverses (there are two) are also unique, with three loops to the bow and large, "lobster-claw" leaves. One variety of Jefferson cent comes with a lettered edge; only two of these are known. The "commoner" Jefferson has some 80 known specimens, along with an unknown number of electrotypes.

Like the Strawberry Leaf cents, the origin of the Jeffersons is uncertain. Some feel they are contemporary counterfeits, as the workmanship is inferior to that of Mint products. Others tend toward the view that they are indeed Mint products, though almost surely experimental and admittedly crude. The prevailing view, however, is that the Jefferson cents were patterns made by John Harper, a private engraver, in an attempt to secure a contract from the Mint for coining cents. But the Mint remained in operation and Harper's dies were confiscated, leaving behind the Jefferson cents as a source of study and speculation for future generations of numismatists.

Moving on from Liberty Cap cents, we encounter the Draped

Busts. 1796 features the popular LIHERTY variety, S-103 and S-104. On this obverse die, the B of LIBERTY was first cut backward and then corrected, giving the letter the appearance of an H. The LIHERTY variety is not rare as cent varieties go (perhaps 500 exist), but because of its popularity it usually commands a good price.

The Mint was under heavy fire from Congress in 1801, a fact reflected in the cents of that year. No fewer than four different dies have the fraction as 1/000, and a fifth was corrected from the same error by having a 1 punched over the erroneous first 0. One of these error dies, however, stands out—the famous 1801 Three Errors. This reverse die contains not one but three obvious blunders: the fraction reads 1/000, the left stem is missing, and UNITED reads as IINITED, as the U was first punched upside-down. That's quite a collection for one die! The 1801 Three Errors is a popular, well-known variety, but how many collectors realize that both 1802 and 1803 feature a three-error die? The die is listed in the 1972 *Guide Book of United States Coins* only as "1802 stemless wreath" and "1803 stemless wreath," yet it does in fact contain three distinct errors: no stems, a double fraction bar, and an extra S below the second S of STATES. This die is far commoner than the 1801 Three Errors; perhaps that is the reason for its comparative lack of notoriety.

One other variety of 1803 deserves mention: the 1803 Large Date, Small Fraction, S-264. This coin, listed in the *Guide Book,* is sought after by date and major variety collectors, die variety collectors both beginning and advanced (most variety collectors begin with the years 1802-1807), and die break enthusiasts (the reverse die fails spectacularly, accounting for the rarity of the variety). Yet in the face of this widespread demand, fewer than 30 specimens of S-264 are known. No other large cent can quite generate the nearly hysterical demand that exists for S-264; one well-known dealer holds 18 different want lists for the coin!

The last year of the Draped Busts, 1807, is known for the Comet variety. Though called a variety, it is actually a die state of S-271, in which linear die flaws strongly resembling a comet trail out behind the head of Liberty. In its final stages, the comet is really quite a sight. Another well-known variety of the year is the 1807/6 Small Overdate, S-272. This variety is much like S-264; it is very rare (about 25 are known) and very much in demand.

As minting equipment and techniques improved, egregious errors and experimental varieties became far less frequent. The late dates, therefore, offer somewhat less in the way of unusual spectacles than do the early dates. Nevertheless, there are a number of fascinating late date varieties. Let's look at some of them.

One weirdo is 1817, Newcomb-16 (Newcomb begins each year with number one; the Sheldon numbers run consecutively). This is the only large cent with 15 stars on the obverse instead of the usual 13. The reason? No one knows—our best guess is simply that a capricious engraver made it on a whim. It is a common coin in circulated condition; an extremely rare coin near Mint State.

What is the rarest major variety in the entire late date series? Most would say the 1839/6, but the real answer is the 1830 Small Letters, N-6. There are probably fewer than 100 specimens of 1830 N-6 extant, nearly all poorly struck, and most of them low grade. Even a VF is very hard to find, and none is known in Mint State.

The most expensive late date cent is the famous and much-disputed overdate, 1839/36, N1. In his description of this coin, Newcomb states: "This variety has long been called the overdate, resembling a figure 9 engraved over a 6. This is an *error* as a die crack connects the loop with ball." But it is Newcomb who is in error, and the proof is simple. In 1837, a change was made from plain to beaded hair cords, and the beaded cords remained in use thereafter. Yet the 1839 N-1 has plain hair cords! The only explanation is the one that fits—the die was originally made in 1836, and the alleged overdate is exactly that.

The 1839/36, with a population of perhaps 150, is nearly as rare as the 1830 Small Letters. The scarcity of the 1839/36 is well accounted for by a dramatic die failure. In its final stage, the obverse die is cracked from rim to rim in a nearly straight line through the nose, eye, and ear. Examples with the crack fully developed are quite rare, and highly prized.

1844 N-2 is better known as 1844/81, but this is really only half the story. In actuality, the entire date was first punched in upside-down, using a four-digit logotype. The erroneous digits were then only partially effaced, and the date punched in properly over their remains. A similar error occurred seven years later, but this time involving only the 18. The result was the 1851/81, N-3. Neither of these errors is particularly rare; of the two, the 1844/81 is somewhat harder to find, especially in top condition.

Our final example of unusual large cents looks anything but unusual. The design is unchanged from the previous year of issue. Both dies are free from error, as is the plain edge. The planchets are perfect in size, weight, and composition, and the striking is superb. What's the catch? Simply this: the coinage of large cents was discontinued by an act of Congress in 1857, and the date on this coin is 1868! Its existence is the final enigma in the large cent series. Although an argument has been made for a pattern issue, the best guess is that like the 1913 Liberty head nickel and the 1885 trade dollar, the 1868 large cent was struck unofficially, and for the sole purpose of providing a rare coin for collectors.

There are many other interesting varieties to be found among the large cents. You can read about them, of course, but why not learn by doing? A very modest expenditure can start a collection of large cents, and introduce you firsthand to this most fascinating series of United States coins. There is even a national club devoted to the study and collecting of the big pennies: the Early American Coppers Club, or EAC. The club publishes a bimonthly newsletter, *Penny-Wise* , that is packed solidly with information about the big cents and the people who collect them. Membership in EAC is open to anyone with an interest in large cents. But I give you fair warning: large cents are addictive. Once the bug bites, it rarely lets go, and you may well find yourself a big penny buff for life. But I wouldn't worry about it—you'll have a lot of company, and it surely is a fun way to go!

From Rare Coin Review No. 14, April-May 1972.

Excessively Excessive

By Q. David Bowers   1983

An article in the *Maine Antique Digest,* by Mary Johnstone, April 1983 issue, reminded the writer that numismatic terminology, like nomenclature used in the antiques business, is wonderfully diverse. Depending upon how you view it, descriptions can be fascinating, inspiring, confusing, redundant, or perhaps a combination of all of these and more!

"Sometimes you can't tell the players without a program, and sometimes you can't read ads for antiques without a translation," Mary Johnstone relates. She goes on to observe that in one recent ad in the *Maine Antique Digest* which featured five items, the word "wonderful" was used four times, "super" was used twice, and the pieces were further described as being "exceptional," "great," and "outstanding."

In numismatics the term "rare" is subject to many interpretations. Most of our readers, we presume, would be more liberal than Ms. Johnstone's observations:

I once read that an item that you would expect to see about twice a year at shows, auctions, or in shops could be called "scarce." If you only see an item once in several years, then that item is "rare."

For the word "unique," we should not have trouble meeting on the common ground of Webster's definition: "Single, sole, being without a like or equal." If you have a unique item, that's it! You have it, no one else does. That one word is the only one needed. By the definition of the word, no degrees are possible. I have seen, however, a peculiar combination of words in antique advertising such as "very unique." Whatever does that mean?

Hans M.F. Schulman, the colorful New York dealer who once wrote a regular column for *Coin World,* showed the writer a coin description, probably from an auction catalogue if memory serves, in which a piece was described as "more unique than the preceding." And, of course, the term "semi-unique" regularly creeps into auction catalogues and other printed offerings. Presumably this means "half-unique" literally, but it is understood to mean "nearly unique," whatever these terms mean.

One of the writer's favorite terms, and one which can be seen with regularity although I have never used it personally (but other catalogu- ers on our staff have), is "excessively rare." To me, this means that the coin is rare to excess or too rare. The piece is rarer than it should be. Presumably "excessively rare" might legitimately apply to a number of things in American numismatics which are rare, but should not be so. An example is the 1794 half dollar in Uncirculated grade. As the first year of issue of this denomination, by all rights a number of them should have been saved, but they weren't. Today the piece is a great rarity, perhaps "excessively rare," for specimens are rarer than they should be. Then there is the 1964 Peace silver dollar. Although 316,076 were struck, "None was preserved or released for circulation." Here, again, is a coin which is rarer than perhaps it should be. Why didn't someone save any? Actually, it seems the 1964 Peace dollar has achieved the *ultimate* degree of rarity; no examples exist.

Sometimes rarity is expressed in terms of personal experience. The rather rhythmic "finest seen by Walter Breen" has meaning, for in his wide travels this well-known expert has seen just about everything. On the other hand, "finest seen by Joe Schlumpf" might not mean much if Joe is a beginning collector.

One of the fun aspects of cataloguing rare coins is having the oppor- tunity to say something "interesting" about them. When I catalogued the 1804 silver dollar, one of America's most famous rarities, for the Garrett Collection we sold for The Johns Hopkins University a few years ago, I could have simply stated my perception of the condition of the coin, its weight in grains, its diameter, and other technical data. All of this would have consumed perhaps two or three sentences. But, no! Here was a piece which was not only a silver dollar, it was *the* silver dollar, a piece which B. Max Mehl referred to years ago as "the king of American coins." Obviously, one has to pay tribute to such numismatic royalty. The result was a multiple-page description which contained the obligatory technical data, but which, more importantly no doubt to the average prospective bidder, transmitted the flavor of the piece, its place in history and its position in numismatics.

In an article which appeared on page 18 of our *Rare Coin Review* No. 47 (1983), Richard A. Bagg, Ph.D. gave his opinion of auction catalogues. Significantly, at least to the present writer who shares Rick Bagg's evaluation, he wrote:

Important catalogues of the 1950s were produced by the New Netherlands Coin Company which were written by the scholarly John J. Ford, Jr., with the assistance of Walter Breen as research associate. These catalogues are to the present writer the most important from that decade as they provide accurate descriptions and a wealth of historical information.

And yet the illustrious catalogues issued by the New Netherlands Coin Company were rich in "flavor" as well. "Excessively rare" cropped up at regular intervals, such as the headline "The Excessively Rare 1824 Half Eagle" used to describe Lot 379 of their June 1957 sale and "The Excessively Rare Quarter Eagle of 1834 with Motto" used in Lot 575 in the same publication. On the other hand, an 1881 $3 piece was listed as being only "extremely rare," while still others were simply described as "rare."

The New Netherlands catalogues excelled with the verbal translation of visual characteristics. One can almost see a 1788 Connecticut copper described as Lot 127 in the June 1958 sale: "Uncirculated. Beneath the 'cartwheel' this cent has a most pleasing blend of light and dark reddish brown delicately mottled with flecks of steel. The planchet is imperfect as usual, but the coin is free of any blemish inflicted after striking. . . ."

The following lot in the same catalogue, also a 1788 Connecticut copper, was described as having a "planchet rough and defective in spots as made (almost entirely on the reverse); a mint clip at lower right. Basically light olive color with a touch or so of dark patina."

Contrasting with the erudite New Netherlands style of cataloguing and presentation is another description noted recently: "1964 Kennedy half dollar, becoming rare." Exactly what does this mean? Is the piece common today but anticipated to be rare tomorrow, or next month, or next year, or a century from now? Considering that nearly 300 *million* were struck, and probably most of these were preserved as novelties, if the 1964 Kennedy half dollar ever becomes "rare," then virtually every other coin in existence will be "excessively rare" by comparison! Rarity indeed is in the eye of the beholder or perhaps in the pen of the owner.

What exactly does *rare* mean? The term cannot be pinned down. Mary Johnstone wrote, as noted, "If you only see an item once in several years, then that item is 'rare.' That seems like a fair estimate."

By that guide very few United States coins could be called rare. The present writer has seen four 1787 Brasher doubloons in the past several years and has sold two of them (including one for $725,000 in November 1979). And yet, virtually any numismatist would state that the coin is deserving of the term "rare" or rare in combination with "very," "exceedingly," or just about any other word you wish to attach.

Rarity means different things to different people. And, rarity does not necessarily equate with value. Most of us would describe a 1909-S V.D.B. cent as "rare," for within the Lincoln cent series from 1909 to date this coin is one of the most difficult to find, along with 1914-D, the 1955 Doubled Die, and several others. In fact, in absolute terms, the 1909-S V.D.B. Lincoln cent is "common" compared to, for example, a relatively inexpensive 1787 Vermont copper coin. A $1.25 broken bank note from our town of Wolfeboro, New Hampshire, a specimen of which was recently exhibited by a Massachusetts dealer, is definitely very rare and may be unique, but when the piece changed hands the price was less than $200. Contrast that to the 1822 half eagle, one of three specimens known, which we sold for $687,500 at the United States Gold Coin Collection Sale in October 1982, or the unique 1870-S $3 piece sold at the same event for the same price.

What does the term *rare* mean in numismatics? Probably a good definition would be that the term could apply to a piece which is infrequently seen by those specializing in the field and, at the same time, is among the top several hardest to find issues within a particular series or field. This definition has its flaws, of course. Is there such a thing as a rare Susan Anthony dollar, for example? Among circulation strikes only a few million were made of the 1981 issues, and I haven't seen many (but I haven't looked for them either), and yet by all standards the piece should be characterized as common. On the other hand, among gold dollars the term "rare" could probably be applied to any Charlotte or Dahlonega Mint issue, Philadelphia issues of the 1860s onwards (with a few exceptions), and a few scattered other issues. Sometimes a coin can be a *condition rarity.* That is, the coin can be common enough in lower grades but very hard to find in top preservation. Time and time again David Akers, in his monumental study of gold coin auction records and frequencies of appearance, pointed out that issues can be very common in worn grades but exceedingly rare or even unknown in Uncirculated preservation.

Popularity sometimes affects rarity. Within the gold dollar series most cataloguers, including the present one, would undoubtedly call *any* gold dollar of the Type II design "rare" although the 1854 and 1855 were made in large quantities. The coins are rare because in terms of other design types of gold issues the Type II is one of the hardest to find.

Of course, coin collecting is fun, and perhaps we should not get too serious about the nomenclature. A poet once asked, "What is so rare as a day in June?" A technical answer might have been a day in April, September, or November, with a day in February being especially rare (but slightly less rare during a leap year).

Mary Johnstone, in her article about antique descriptions, noted that "superlatives are fun but are hard to pin down." She noted that technically oriented advertisements "are accurate and easy to pin down, *but are not much fun to read.*"

In today's world, numismatics provides a ray of sunshine. While our clients collect for a diversity of reasons, including study, investment, and history, certainly the aspect of *fun* ranks as being important. At least it should be.

From Rare Coin Review No. 48, June-July 1983.

Memories of a Rare Coin Dealer

By Q. David Bowers | 1972

The other day I opened a blue and white airmail packet from a dealer friend in London. Responding to my request as to what he might have in interesting United States coins, he sent me a prize: an attractively toned, mint-condition dime of 1805—a coin which, no doubt, had been taken to England years earlier by someone returning from America. The little 1805 dime, a coin which was sold to a want list customer a day or two later, reminded me of some of the good times I have had in England.

During the early 1960s I spent quite a bit of time in England, particularly in London. In fact, it is probably accurate to say I've spent more time in London than in any other major city in the world—excepting, of course, cities in which I have lived. Sometimes Jim Ruddy, my partner in the firm of Bowers and Ruddy, went along on the trip. Other times I went to England alone.

The reasons for going to England were twofold; to buy United States coins and to buy English coins. Although it might not sound particularly logical at first, there is a good reason—in fact, several of them—why American coins are, or were, to be found in England.

In my *Coins and Collectors* book I touched upon the early interest in England in collecting American coins: "When the new United States Mint at Philadelphia commenced coinage in 1793, it was only natural that many English collectors would take notice and strive to obtain representative pieces. After all, just a few years earlier the American colonies were English possessions. Many choice United States copper and silver coins found their way into English cabinets. Today many of the finest known American coins of the 1793-1800 era have crossed the Atlantic twice."

Another reason for finding United States coins in England is that many American coins were acquired as souvenirs—pocket change as they were at the time—by Englishmen who visited America on vacation and sightseeing trips. While American citizens were busy carving a nation out of the wilderness, England was the very model of sophisticated civilization. What more adventuresome trip could be imagined than a visit to the American "wild West" or even to the comparatively settled eastern cities? Charles Dickens, for one, visited America (in 1842) and returned to delight Englishmen with his tales of "roughing it."

Another less heralded visitor from England, but a much more important one from a numismatic viewpoint, was an ancestor of Lord St. Oswald. This unnamed gentleman had the numismatic good fortune (for his descendants!) to visit the United States in the 1790s. To remember his visit he brought back a few of the novel-appearing American 1794 dollars, and a few other souvenirs. These moldered away in a large country estate until the early 1960s when a descendant, Lord St. Oswald, found the coins and brought them to the salesrooms of Christie's in London. What followed would make a good story in itself—but suffice it to say that Christie's salesroom on the appointed day had as many prominent English and American dealers in attendance as have ever been in one place at one time! The prices, spectacular then (the Uncirculated 1794 dollars brought about $12,000 apiece, if memory serves), appear a bit more reasonable now; they would even be bargains today.

Edward VIII's Threepence—and Other Coins

Occasionally a coin dealer will get what my Copenhagen friend Claes O. Friberg calls a *possession desire*—a strong urge to own something. I am no exception, and it is nice to mentally notch a little counting stick as great rarities are handled. The ownership of numismatic milestones, even if they are owned only for a few days or weeks, is very gratifying. You've sensed my feelings on this, no doubt, if you've read my enthusiastic descriptions of the famed 1907 MCMVII Extremely High Relief $20, 1838-O half dollar, 1894-S dime, 1876-CC 20-cent piece, 1827 quarter, etc. in any *Review Coin Review* issue and or auction catalogue.

Well, in the early 1960s Jim Ruddy and I became enamored with English coins. At the time, there were four major coin dealers in England: Messrs. Spink, Seaby, and Baldwin, who held forth from their time-honored premises in London, and a few hours' ride from London, Fred Jeffrey in Wiltshire. It was Jeffrey, incidentally, who suggested the queen-on-horseback design which was used for the English coronation crown of 1953. If a fifth (and sixth) dealer were to be nominated to the list, it would be Corbett & Hunter, a pair of friendly numismatists who did business in the ancient St. Nicholas Buildings in Newcastle-upon-Tyne in the north of England. I visited there many times and was usually rewarded with some interesting coins.

The first English coin convention, or "coin fair" as they are called, was yet to be held. The first popularly circulated coin magazine was yet to be published. Coin collecting wasn't "popular" in the public sense. The dealers did a brisk trade with established numismatists who knew what they were looking for among ancient Greek and Roman coins, rare English crowns, etc. The filling of "penny boards," the popular American pastime which has spawned so many numismatists, was unknown. Who cared about collecting farthings, halfpennies, or pennies from circulation? Few, if any.

Of course, all of this is changed now. An Uncirculated English 1919-KN penny, a rare issue coined at the curiously named Kings Norton Mint—a coin which might have cost all of two or three dollars in 1960—would cause spirited competition if it came up for sale today.

Jim Ruddy and I read all we could about English coins—and then set about building a stock of them. English coins are usually collected by rulers—kings and queens—as well as by dates. Of all modern rulers, King Edward VIII was the most ephemeral. His abdication from the royal throne, before his coronation in fact, to marry Mrs. Wallis Warfield Simpson is one of the great love stories of our time. When the former king, known as the Duke of Windsor in his later years, died earlier this year it brought back some memories of one of the most famous of all English coins: the 12-sided brass threepence bearing his portrait.

An extensive coinage for the soon-to-be-crowned king was contemplated, and pieces of various denominations were struck bearing Edward VIII's portrait. The now-familiar 12-sided brass threepence was a new coin shape and size at the time, and it was deemed advisable to give a few pieces, perhaps a dozen in all, to various manufacturers of coin-operated machines so the coins could be tested for use. Or so the story goes.

The coronation never took place, and what few coins of Edward VIII minted were destroyed—except for those given to coin machine manufacturers for testing. The result is that fewer than a dozen English coins bearing the portrait of Edward VIII are known today—and these are brass threepence pieces.

Jim Ruddy asked many collectors and dealers in England about a specimen of the Edward VIII pieces, but none could be located. Finally we learned of a man from Yorkshire who owned one of the coins and who was fond of showing it in his local pub. After much correspondence and negotiation, the owner of the coin journeyed to London with his prize. The money, carefully drawn from the bank beforehand, was ready as he and several relatives visited us in our suite at the newly completed London Hilton Hotel. They could hardly believe their good fortune as they counted out their money. "Why would anyone pay such a price?" the owner asked. "I never thought you would accept!" the owner asked. We were just as pleased—for the elusive 1937 Edward VIII brass threepence was ours! We had never seen one before—and now we owned one. Shortly after we returned to America, our "possession desire" fulfilled, we offered it for sale. It is now the centerpiece in the fabulous museum collection assembled by Mr. Carl Nickel of Alberta, Canada.

Another highlight of my trips to England was meeting noted numismatist C. Wilson Peck. Mr. Peck, a seemingly tireless and very dedicated numismatic scholar, wrote the monumental *English Copper, Tin, and Bronze Coins* tome—a reference book which has never been equaled in its field.

During one of my visits to Mr. Peck's home, he asked me what I thought his famed 1954 English penny was worth. I had heard of the coin, of course—and it was on my list of coins I would like to own someday. Over a million English pennies bearing the portrait of Queen Elizabeth II were coined in 1953. In the following year only a few, perhaps just one, were minted! The only known English penny of 1954 was the one in in Mr. Peck's collection. He recounted how he had purchased it a few years earlier from Spink & Son, London dealers, and how happy he was that no other 1954 English pennies had come to light since then!

I had no answer to Mr. Peck's query as to the worth of his 1954 penny. What is such a coin worth? Literally, it is priceless—for once it is sold, no amount of money can secure another. I asked Mr. Peck to name a valuation—which he did. To my surprise he then asked, "Would you pay that much?"

To his surprise I answered, "Yes!"

The agreement to buy the coin was made on the spot—and back to the hotel I went with the prize. I showed it to Jim Ruddy, who was busy with another gentleman when I entered the room. Not wanting to pause from the middle of his transaction, Jim looked at the 1954 penny and quietly asked what it cost. He was amazed at the price!

At the same time I purchased from Mr. Peck a Proof Bahama penny of 1806. I paid five pounds (about $14 at the time) for it. The Bahama penny, with its legends romantically referring to the expulsion of pirates from that Atlantic isle, had always been one of my favorite coins—and Jim saw my enthusiasm about this glittering Proof. With the price paid for the unique 1954 English penny still in his mind, Jim asked me: "How much did it cost?"

"Five," was my reply—with obvious enthusiasm, for I thought it was quite a bargain for just five pounds.

"Good luck—you'll need it!" was Jim's comeback. Later he told me he thought that "five" meant five hundred pounds!

Some English Travels

I never could get used to the English system of driving on the left-hand side of the road. My first attempt at it—a brief drive around the hotel—nearly ended in disaster, so from then on I found it far more expedient and infinitely safer to hire a chauffeur.

Before visiting England I would advertise in several of the publications about antiques (there were no general-circulation magazines specifically about coins) and would write letters to various collectors and dealers in England. The result was that I could roughly map out a "tour" through the English provinces—stopping to conduct business in a dozen or so places along the way.

The experiences on these trips bring back many fond memories. I viewed the trips as adventures, not as numismatic business. And, in a way, they were adventures. And they were quite interesting.

I have always had an insatiable desire to learn about various things—and to me, old English castles are among the most fascinating things I've ever seen. I remember that my driver and I once hand-carried in briefcases one of the nicest English collections I ever purchased—hand-carried it through the ancient ruins of Middleham Castle during a rainstorm!

During another visit my driver and I went to Torquay, a resort town on the southern coast of England. We arrived at the Grand Hotel (I think that was the name of the impressive-looking Victorian establishment) around six in the evening. I approached the front desk of the Grand and saw an empty guest register. I wrote down my name and address and then asked, "How many people are staying here this evening?"

"You are the only guest, sir," was the reply in the most formal English possible. It seemed that my visit was during a period of particularly bad weather in mid-December, and no one in his right mind would pick that time to visit an English seacoast resort! The place remained open, however, for tradition's sake and in anticipation of a busy season during the Christmas-New Year's week which was approaching.

I checked into my room, which for some reason was down a very long corridor on the third floor, and then went downstairs to the main dining room. A waiter, who had been formally standing at attention along one wall, strode briskly over to show me my seat and provide me with a menu.

I noticed the day's date, (December 19th, I believe) was printed on the menu. "Why does the hotel have printed menus each day when business is slow?" I asked. "Why not have a 'standard' menu for the off-season? It seems to me that this would be a bit less expensive than printing a menu just for one guest!"

This befuddled the waiter, who was obviously not accustomed to the casual ways of visiting Americans, and he retired hastily to a far wall of the dining room while I made my dinner selection. When he came over to take my order I told him he could come to my table and have a cup of coffee and keep me company after he was finished serving. "Oh, no—I couldn't do anything like that!" he said, blushing.

After finishing my solo supper I took a copy of the latest *Time* magazine, which I had foresightedly acquired in London, with me into a nearby lounge. I sprawled out comfortably on an overstuffed chair and began to read the latest news. Within a few minutes a man sprang up from a nearby chair and went up onto a stage. He began playing the piano. Seeking some conversation, I went over to him. "You play well. Why do you pick this place, with nobody around, to play music—or are you just practicing?" I asked.

"I am playing for you," he replied. "Our adverts [English for "advertisements"] mention that we have 'live entertainment,' so here I am!"

Despite my protests that he didn't have to play just for me, he did so anyway—so for the next half hour I heard music from *South Paci-*

fic—"Americans like these tunes," he said.

The next day I was up bright and early. In the town of Torquay I purchased a splendid collection of English shillings—a group including the extremely rare 1952 (a coin of which fewer than a half dozen exist!) and the famous Dorrien & Magens issue of 1798. The collection went to the United States with me a week or so later. At the office we were very busy (as it seems we always are!), so the collections of English shillings was put into a bank vault and nearly forgotten. When Douglas Liddell, director and representative of Spink & Son, visited us in the United States a year or so later, I remembered the shilling collection. It was retrieved from the bank, spread out on a table for viewing, duly inspected and purchased by Mr. Liddell—and shortly thereafter, was on its way back to England!

A Grandfather Clock

On another trip I spent an afternoon in Huddersfield, a textile-milling town located in the province of Yorkshire. I was there on the invitation of an English collector who had earlier written to me in America about buying his collection.

Early in the afternoon I arrived at his home—a beautiful stone and masonry home with a sharply peaked roof and with diamond-shaped, leaded panes in the windows. I was shown into the living room by the collector's wife and was offered a cup of coffee. Contrary to my earlier thoughts, I found that coffee is a more popular drink with Englishmen—at least with the English numismatists I visited—than is tea! The owner of the collection, I was told, was busy in his study and would be down to see me in a few minutes. While seated in the living room, I spied an absolutely magnificent grandfather clock majestically occupying a distant corner. An incurable collector of antiques, I walked over to look at it more closely. The face was of engraved brass with a pierced metalwork overlay. The case was of rich woods decorated with carvings and inlay. It was a masterpiece!

My host entered the room, and I complimented him on the grandfather clock and asked about its history. He told me all about it and was pleased I had admired one of his favorite possessions.

The talk soon changed to the purpose of my visit—numismatics—and the clock was forgotten. From some storage place in a distant room tray after tray of coins were brought to a table in the living room. I made offers for the collection section by section, and in an hour or two the collection was mine. The collection was mostly comprised of crowns, including Proof examples of the rare 1826, 1831, and 1853 issues. The only United States coins in the group were Proof coins of 1880—a copper, nickel, and silver Proof set. I wrote out a check for the purchase of the collection and then stayed an hour or so longer to converse about various things. As the time was then late, my driver had to go full speed ahead to make it to our reserved hotel room in time.

When I returned to America an airmail letter on the familiar blue paper used by the English was waiting for me. I opened it and learned it was from the daughter of the Huddersfield numismatist whose collection I had purchased two weeks earlier.

"My father died on Sunday, the day after you were here," she wrote. "You were the last person he talked to, apart from members of our family. Right before he died he asked me to write to you and ask you if you would accept his grandfather clock—the one you admired so much—as a gift, so I am now doing so."

I didn't know what to say, but after thinking it over I decided to accept the generous gift. The collection I purchased in Huddersfield was a magnificent one, and I enjoyed the company of its owner during my visit. The clock would be a wonderful memento of the occasion and of its fine former owner. Accordingly, I wrote back with my acceptance and gave the London address of my shipping agent there, Davies, Turner & Co. Not wanting to cause the family any extra expense, I told them I would have Davies, Turner collect the clock next time they had a truck in the Huddersfield area.

A month or so later I received a letter from Davies, Turner & Co.. "We don't know this American fellow, so why should we give him this valuable clock?" said another relative of the owner when Davies, Turner called for it. So, where the beautiful clock is now, I don't know.

From Rare Coin Review *No. 16, October-December 1972.*

From Wampum to Coin

By George Francis Dow | 1985

The early settlers of New England had little coinage for circulation and were driven to the necessity of using the produce of the soil and the livestock from their pastures as their media of exchange. Peltry also was one of the first and for many years the principal article of currency. It was offered in great abundance by the Indians who were very ready to barter it for beads, knives, hatchets, blankets, and especially for powder, shot guns, and "strong water."

In most of the Colonies the wampum of the Indians also was extensively used and frequently was paid into the treasury in payment of taxes. So, also, were cattle and corn as is shown by numerous enactments of the Great and General Court of the Massachusetts Bay. Musket balls were also current and were made legal tender by order of the Court which decreed "that musket bullets of a full bore shall pass current for a farthing apiece provided that no man be compelled to take more than 12 pence at a time of them." In Virginia, tobacco was used for currency and "from 100 to 150 pounds of it brought many a man a good wife."

The Indian wampum was perhaps the most convenient currency available. It is described by Roger Williams who, perhaps, had a better knowledge of it than most of the early colonists. He says: "It is of two kinds which the Indians make of the stem or the stock of the periwinkle after all the shell is broken off. [The periwinkle is a mollusk, more common south of Cape Cod than along the shores of Massachusetts Bay.] Of this kind, six of the small beads, which they make with holes to string upon their bracelet, are current with the English for a penny. The other kind is black, inclined to a blue shade, which is made of the shell of a fish [that is, a mollusk] which some of the English call henspoquahoc [now known as the hen-clam or quahaug] and of this description three are equal to an English penny. One fathom of this stringed money is worth five shillings."

To show the intimate relation of this Indian money to our early history, it appears that even Harvard College accepted it for tuition fees and otherwise; for in 1641 a trading company, chartered to deal with the Indians in furs and wampum, was required to relieve the College of its abundance of this odd currency and redeem it, "provided they were not obliged to take more than 25 pounds of it at any one time." The thrifty Dutch at New Amsterdam, however, took advantage of the scarcity of legitimate currency and the corresponding demand for the wampum and established factories where they made it in such vast quantities that the market was broken and the value of wampum rapidly decreased.

The great source of metallic currency for New England in those earliest days was the West India Islands, and much silver brought from there was later coined into Pine Tree shillings and sixpences. Governor Winthrop, in 1639, tells of a "small bark from the West Indies, one Capt. Jackson in her, with a commission from the Westminster Company to take prizes from the Spanish. He brought much wealth in money, plate, indigo, and sugar." But metallic money became so scarce that by 1640 there was but little in the colonies and the greatest difficulty existed in making payments for goods or the wages of servants. In one instance, in Rowley, "The master was forced to sell a pair of his oxen to pay his servant's wages and so told the servant he could keep him no longer, not knowing how to pay him the next year. The servant answered him that he would [continue to] serve him for more of his cattle. But what shall I do, said the master, when all my cattle are gone? The servant replied, why, then you shall serve me and you shall then have your cattle again."

Various attempts were made to establish values to certain coins, more or less ficticious, but this failed to relieve the situation and finally, to obtain a more stable basis, the Massachusetts General Court adopted a currency of its own and the Pine Tree money appeared, shortly preceded by the more rude and more easily counterfeited New England shillings and sixpences, that bore on one side the letters N.E. within a small circle and on the other side the denomination in Roman numerals. These primitive coins were manufactured between 1650 and 1652, and were superceded by the true Oak and Pine Tree pieces manufactured after that date. The simple irregular form of the N.E.

coins rendered them easy prey to the counterfeiter and the clipper, and the design of the newer coins, covering the whole surface of the planchet, was a protection against both dangers. The N.E. shilling is now a rare coin and likewise the sixpence, while the threepence is rarer still, but two or three genuine examples are presently known to exist.

There are two distinct forms of the so-called Pine Tree currency, the one bearing on the obverse a representation of a tree resembling an oak, or as some say, a willow; the other with the true pine tree. It is thought that the ruder pieces bearing the oak tree design were the first coined and that the more perfect pine tree money was issued later. At any rate both Oak and Pine Tree pieces, shillings, sixpences, and threepences, all bear the same date, 1652. But this money was issued continuously until 1686 without a change of the date, it is said to avoid interference from the English government, the coining of money by the colonists being a distinct violation of the royal prerogative. By the retention of the original date it was thought to deceive the authorities at home into the belief that the violation of the laws ceased as it began, in 1652. In 1662, however, a two-penny piece was minted bearing the oak tree design and hence it is natural to suppose that the pieces bearing the true pine tree design were the last coined and not issued until after 1662.

One of the traditions connected with the Pine or Oak Tree money is the story that Sir Thomas Temple, who was a real friend of the colonists, in 1662, showed some of the pieces to the King at the council table in London, when King Charles demanded upon what authority these colonists had coined money anyway and sought to have orders sent to prohibit any further issues. "But," responded Sir Thomas, "this tree is the oak which saved your majesty's life and which your loyal subjects would perpetuate." Sir Thomas of course referred to the episode of Boscobel in which Charles II escaped his enemies by hiding in the branches of an oak. This it is said so pleased the King that he dropped the subject and coining of Pine Tree money proceeded merrily, as before, for 25 years longer.

The master of the Mint was John Hull who lived in Boston where Pemberton Square now opens from Tremont Street and where later was the famous garden and residence of Gardner Green, Esq. The mint house, 16 feet square and 10 feet high, was built on land belonging to Hull in the rear of his house. Robert Sanderson, a friend of Hull, was associated with him in making the Pine Tree money. It is not known how they divided their profit, but they received one shilling sixpence for each 20 shillings coined, and as it is estimated that Pine Tree money to the amount of 5 million dollars in value was made during the 34 years it was issued, the commissions received must have been very large and the statement that the dowry, said to have been 30,000 pounds, given to Hull's daughter at her marriage, appears reasonable. That the girl, plump as she is reported to have been, actually weighed down the dowry in shillings, is, of course, absurd as that amount in silver would weigh over 6,000 pounds rating a silver pound as weighing four ounces at that time.

Hawthorne's description of what is said to have taken place on that occasion is too vivid a picture to be overlooked. He relates that Captain Hull was appointed to manufacture the Pine Tree money and had about one shilling out of every 20 to pay him for the trouble of making them. Hereupon all the old silver in the colony was handed over to Captain John Hull. The battered silver cans and tankards, I suppose, and silver buckles and broken spoons and silver hilts of swords that figured at court—all such articles were doubtless thrown into the melting pot together.

The magistrates soon began to suspect that the mintmaster would have the best of the bargain and they offered him a large sum of money if he would but give up that 20th shilling which he was continually dropping into his own pocket. But Captain Hull declared himself perfectly satisfied with the shilling. And well he might be, for so diligently did he labor that in a few years, his pockets, his money bags, and his strong box were overflowing with Pine Tree shillings.

Then Samuel Sewall, afterwards the famous Judge Sewall of the days of witchcraft fame, came a courting to Hull's daughter. Betsy was a fine and hearty damsel and having always fed heartily on pumpkin pies, doughnuts, Indian puddings, and other Puritan dainties, she was as round and plump as pudding herself.

"Yes, you may take her," said Captain Hull, to her lover, young Sewall, "and you'll find her a heavy burden enough." Hawthorne describes the wedding and the costumes of the contracting parties and their friends, and Captain Hull he "supposes," rather improbably one would think, however, "dressed in a plum-colored coat all the bottoms of which were made of Pine Tree shillings. The buttons of his waistcoat were of sixpences and the knees of his small clothes were buttoned with silver threepences. . .and as to Betsy herself, she was blushing with all her might, and looked like a full-blown peony or a great red apple."

When the marriage ceremony was over, at a whispered word from Captain Hull, a large pair of scales was lugged into the room, such as wholesale merchants use for weighing bulky commodities, and quite a bulky commodity was now to be weighed in them. "Daughter Betsy," said the mintmaster, "get into one side of these scales." Miss Betsy—or Mrs. Sewall as we must now call her—did as she was bid and again the servants tugged, this time bringing a huge ironbound oaken chest which being opened proved to be full to the brim with bright Pine Tree shillings fresh from the Mint. At Captain Hull's command the servants heaped double handfuls of shillings into one side of the scales, while Betsy remained in the other. Jingle, jingle, went the shillings as handful after handful was thrown in, 'till, plump and ponderous as she was, they fairly weighed the young lady from the floor. "There, son Sewall," cried the honest mintmaster, resuming his seat, "take these shillings for my daughter's portion. Use her kindly and thank heaven for her. It's not every wife who's worth her weight in silver."

However interesting the story may be of the plump girl sitting in one pan of the scales as shillings were thrown into the other, as depicted in Hawthorne's version of the affair, we must be permitted to consider that the time has cast a halo around the mintmaster's daughter and increased her avoirdupois and her dowry.

Massachusetts was the only New England colony to coin silver but close upon the date of the issue of the first Pine Tree money came the Maryland shilling, sixpence, groat and penny, the last in copper. These bear no date but appeared about 1659, the dies having been made in England.

Numerous coins were later made in the colonies, either intended for regular circulation or as tokens privately issued, among which are the Granby coppers—rude halfpennies—made in 1737 by one John Higley, the blacksmith, at Granby, Connecticut. They were made of soft copper which was dug at Granby and are never found in very good condition.

The word dollar is the English form of the German word thaler, and the origin of the thaler is as follows: In the year 1519, Count Schlick of Bohemia issued silver coins weighing one ounce each and worth 113 cents. They were coined at Joachimsthal, that is, James's Valley or dale, hence they became known as "Joachismthalers," soon shortened to thalers. Through trade with the Dutch these coins came into England in the 16th century and are referred to sometimes as "dalers."

But the dollar came to the American continent not through the Dutch or English but through the Spanish. This was due to the extent of the Spanish Empire in the 16th and 17th centuries and also to the great quantities of silver which Spain drew from her mines in Mexico and South America. The Spanish coin was, strictly speaking, a peso, better known as a "piece of eight," because it was equal to eight reals (royals). As it was the same value, the name dollar was given to the piece of eight about the year 1690.

The most famous Spanish dollar was known as the pillar dollar, because it had on one side two pillars, representing the Pillars of Hercules, the classical name for the Strait of Gibraltar, and this Spanish dollar was common in America at the time of the War of Independence.

From Rare Coin Review No. 57, *Autumn 1985, reprinted from Chapter XII, "From Wampum to Paper Money," in* Every Day Life in the Massachusetts Bay Colony, *published by The Society for the Preservation of New England Antiquities, Boston, 1935.*

The Money Pit

By D'Arcy O'Connor   1970

OAK ISLAND, Nova Scotia—Dan Blankenship admits that most of his friends have written him off as "some kind of a nut."

At first glance, it would seem they have good reason. Mr. Blankenship has spent most of the past five years and about $80,000 of his own money digging for buried treasure on this desolate, spruce covered island about 45 miles west of Halifax. All he has to show for it so far are a few bits of metal, some buds from oak trees, chips of wood and pieces of china, not to mention infected black fly bites covering both arms. But the 47-year old Miami contractor also has an unshakable conviction that by the end of the summer he and his associates will accomplish what hundreds of searchers have been unable to do during the past 175 years—solve the mystery of Oak Island and perhaps make themselves millionaires as well.

The mystery centers on a maze of underground man-made workings known to exist on the island at depths running down to more than 200 feet. Who dug the shafts is not known. The most prevalent theory is that they are the work of 17th-century pirates, possibly Captain William Kidd or Henry Morgan.

Vikings, Incas, or Buccaneers

Other theories suggest that Vikings, Peruvian Incas, Spanish buccaneers, or even Leonardo da Vinci engineered the intricate workings. In any case, it's clear the project was built to hide something of great value, and estimates of the amount of treasure presumed to be buried on Oak Island run as high as $30 million. But not a penny has been uncovered to date.

Mr. Blankenship is not alone in his fascination with Oak Island. Last year, after years of working alone, he joined 24 other Canadian and United States businessmen in a syndicate formed to pursue exploration of the island. Many of the other members had, like Mr. Blankenship, made earlier efforts on their own to unravel the mystery.

The syndicate is known as Triton Alliance, Ltd., and it is the best-equipped group ever to tackle the island; the men who formed the syndicate pooled $520,000 to finance their operations. Headed by David Tobias, 46-year old president of Jonergin Co., a Montreal label manufacturer, Triton has spent the past three summers conducting exploratory drill tests on the 128-acre island. The recently completed tests have "absolutely convinced us that there are original shafts and chambers" under the island's clay surface, says Tobias. He rates the group's chances of finding any treasure at about one in four but adds that "as long as we can prove who was responsible for the workings and for what purpose they were made, we'd be very happy."

George L. Jennison, past president of the Toronto Stock Exchange and a member of the Triton syndicate, agrees that his participation is primarily "to satisfy this curiosity I've had ever since I heard about Oak Island as a boy." The 64-year old stockbroker sees the project as "an interesting speculative venture, so I thought I'd take a flyer on it. Who knows, maybe we'll strike it lucky and find some treasure."

Two Farmers' Discovery

Existence of the underground workings was discovered by two farmers on the island in 1795, when they noticed a slight depression in the ground at the foot of a large oak tree and found evidence that the brush had been cleared away some years before. Digging down, the two men discovered that the soil had been previously worked and that they were standing in a refilled shaft seven feet across.

At the 10-foot level, the men struck a platform of oak logs spread across the shaft and imbedded in the hard clay sides of the pit. They broke through the logs and continued to dig, encountering similar log platforms at each 10-foot interval to a depth of 30 feet. At this point they were unable to proceed further without help, but because of local skepticism and superstition concerning the island they weren't able to obtain assistance.

Work on the project wasn't resumed until 1804, when a treasure hunting syndicate was formed to continue the digging. This group continued to strike oak log platforms every 10 feet, as well as layers of charcoal, coconut fiber matting, an inscribed stone and a putty-like substance. At the 93-foot level the diggers hammered a crowbar into the earth and struck a hard impenetrable substance five feet below. They were certain it was a large metal object, but because night was coming on they decided to wait 'till morning to resume digging. The following morning, however, they returned to find the pit filled with 60 feet of sea water.

Their primitive pumps were unable to reduce the water level, and although they dug other shafts nearby with the intention of cross-tunneling to the so-called money pit, these, too, immediately filled with water once the money pit was intersected. It was later discovered that a man-made flood tunnel intersected the money pit at about the 100-foot level and that it ran 520 feet to a cove in the island where it fanned out underwater into five well-constructed "box drains." Made of rocks cemented together, these units include catch basins that collect silt and prevent it from washing into the flood tunnel.

Flooding Remains a Problem

The existence of this tunnel thwarted later attempts to dig directly into the money pit. In 1897, however, its path was traced and the flow of water through it blocked. It was found to be two and one-half feet wide and four feet high, with a drop of 22½ degrees as it angled toward the money pit. Nevertheless, flooding, which even a 1,000 gallon-a-minute pump could not control has continued to be the main problem encountered in more recent digs. The island's hard clay soil ruled out the possibility of natural seepage, and in 1898 it was discovered that at least one other flood tunnel led from the south shore of the island into the money pit at about the 150-foot level.

It's thought there may be other flood tunnels as well, and all attempts to pump out shafts in the immediate money pit area have been tantamount to trying to bail out the surrounding ocean. Large quantities of coconut fiber have been found buried in the money pit area and in the cover containing the box drains. In 1916 a sample of this material was submitted to the Smithsonian Institution for analysis. The institution reported that the specimen was "undoubtedly from the fibrous husks of a coconut." The fiber, which was used by early sailing ships as dunnage for packing cargo, is believed to be Caribbean in origin.

Stone is Lost

The inscribed stone found at about the 90-foot level of the money pit was lost in 1919. Around the turn of the century, however, a professor of languages as Dalhousie College in Halifax had claimed to have interpretted the strange characters and numerals of the 175-pound stone as stating: "Ten feet below two million pounds lie buried."

The deep underground workings, with their intersecting flood tunnels presumably designed to keep intruders from reaching whatever is buried on the island, have been described by mining and engineering experts as an incredible and ingenious engineering feat. It's estimated that it would have taken several hundred men more than two years to have completed the project with pre 16th-century tools and technology.

The many failures by searchers to solve the puzzle prompted author A. Hyatt Verrill to describe Oak Island in his book *Lost Treasures* as "perhaps the most mysterious treasure in the entire world, a treasure which, though known to exist, has never been recovered, and which is undoubtedly the most remarkable concealed treasure known."

Today the eastern end of the uninhabited island is a rabbit warren of shafts and tunnels dug by previous searchers over the years. The money pit area now resembles a scarred battlefield. Trees have been hacked away to provide timbers for shafts; piles of dirt, rusting metal shaft casings and abandoned equipment are scattered about; and huge gaping water-filled craters testify to the work of scores of treasure seekers over the years. The island, situated in Nova Scotia's picturesque Mahone Bay, is now connected to the mainland by a half-mile-long causeway built several years ago to provide access for heavy digging equipment.

A total of 15 major assaults have been made on Oak Island, many of them by stock subscription finance companies. Even Franklin D. Roosevelt, whose family owned a nearby summer residence, was a partner in a 1909 syndicate formed to recover the treasure. Most of these groups were able to add various pieces to the Oak Island puzzle while digging shafts and tunnels in the money pit area. Each one of them, however, encountered the problem of flooding as the various tunnels approached the actual money pit.

Even less successful were the various individual searchers over the years who came armed with "authentic" pirate maps, divining rods, radar sets, and even seance-inspired guidance.

$1.5 Million, Six Deaths

Triton's Mr. Tobias estimates that previous searchers have spent more than $1.5 million. Moroever, six deaths are known to have resulted from the search, four of them in 1965 when workers in a shaft were overcome by carbon monoxide fumes from a gasoline powered pump motor.

All previous major searches have been abandoned for lack of money—not because of any lack of evidence that there was something in the pit. Indeed, many tantalizing clues have been unearthed. These include the hugh quantities of coconut fiber matting, links of gold chain, pieces of hand-hewn wood that have been carbon dated to about 1575, a 1598 Spanish coin, the inscribed stone, and a piece of old parchment recovered from a depth of 153 feet. Other drilling and core samplings in the water-filled money pit have indicated the presence of wooden chests filled with loose metal as well as an oak box surrounded by concrete and an iron plate deep in the pit.

Skeptics point to the fact that the island has been worked since 1795 and that many of the so-called clues could have been "salted" by previous searchers. Triton, however, has come up with evidence it considers incontestible.

Below Bedrock Level

Under the supervision of outside consulting engineers, the company has put down 75 drill holes in the vicinity of the money pit. Most of these reached below the bedrock level, which begins at about 165 feet and goes for about 40 more feet, and it's known that no previous searchers ever sank a shaft this far down. Core samples taken from beneath bedrock have yielded tiny oak buds, bits of china, pieces of brass and low carbon steel, and traces of spruce and hemlock pollen. Most of this material was found suspended in "puddled" clay, a putty-like substance that geologists and mining engineers say was commonly used in underground workings as a water seal before the development of concrete.

Several of the drill holes hit definite cavities 8 to 10 feet deep beginning below bedrock—or more than 200 feet below the surface—and core samples showed that the cavities contained ceilings of wood planking several inches thick. The carbon-dating of the wood to 1575, plus or minus 85 years, has helped convince Triton engineers they have struck the timbers and crib-work of the original man-made chambers. Within the next few weeks Triton intends to begin its own excavation program. The company plans to sink a vertical shaft into bedrock in the undisturbed soil adjacent to the money pit area. From there, horizontal shafts will fan out to reach the cavities discovered in the drilling program. Mr. Tobias is certain that the shafting will unravel the mystery "within three months." If not, "then that's it," he says with a shrug. "We'll have to pull out."

Waiting 74 Years

Melbourne R. Chappell, an 83-year old Sydney, Nova Scotia engineer, is probably more anxious than anybody to see the mystery solved. A Triton partner and the current owner of the island, he has been waiting 74 years to satisfy his curiosity, ever since his father was associated with an 1896 search group. Mr. Chappell also holds "treasure trove" rights to the island, which give him and his partners exclusive rights to dig on the site, providing that 10% of any treasure found is turned over to the provincial government.

While the Triton syndicate members are all convinced they are on the verge of an exciting archaeological discovery, and may perhaps get rich in the process, they hold divergent views on what they expect to find. Mr. Blankenship doubts that pirates had anything to do with the project, and he has "a strong hunch" that the workings are pre-Columbian. Mr. Chappell thinks the secret of the island "might well be the Inca treasure."

The Inca theory is shared by many previous Oak Island searchers who cite the fact that the Incas were skillful architects and would be more capable than pirates of engineering the complex project. They contend the island probably contains long-lost treasure of Tumbez, an ancient city on the northern tip of Peru.

Treasure of Tumbez

According to 16th-century Spanish documents, Francisco Pizarro, the Spanish adventurer and conqueror of Peru, visited Tumbez in 1528 and decided to carry away all of its treasures. However, while he was on his way back to Spain to gather together a force large enough to capture the city, Inca rulers had all of the city's gold and silver riches placed on ships, intending to remove them to safety somewhere in the Caribbean. According to the documents, the expedition ran into hurricanes that forced the ships up the North American coast. They are said to have found shelter at some unknown point far northward where they buried the Tumbez treasure.

Tobias, on the other hand, thinks the group may uncover a pirate communal bank, similar to one discovered in Haiti in 1949. This, in effect, is a large underground bank vault engineered and used cooperatively by several bands of pirates, and probably dug with slave labor. In the Haitian discovery, which yielded about $17,000 in Spanish coins, several corridors led from the main vault into smaller chambers, and it's believed these served as "safety deposit boxes" for the individual pirates. The mail vault was reached by a vertical shaft, and, like the Oak Island money pit, was booby-trapped with several flood channels.

A further similarity between the Haitian and Oak Island workings was the recent discovery by Blankenship of a large hand-chiseled heart-shaped stone buried in the area of the original flood tunnel. A stone just like it was found in one of the corridors leading from the main vault of the Haitian communal bank.

An Elaborate Decoy

Another theory holds that the money pit and its intersecting flood tunnels constitute an elaborate decoy, designed to lure treasure seekers away from some large treasure buried a few feet underground elsewhere on the island.

Chappell says he has received "dozens of letters from all over the world" whose authors claim to know exactly where the treasure is buried as well as who buried it. Some of their stories are rather farfetched. "One guy even told me he knew for sure that Leonardo da Vinci designed the workings," adds Mr. Chappell with a slight smile.

But no matter what their pet theories as to the origin of the workings, the Triton syndicate partners are united by an almost fanatic determination to solve the mystery of Oak Island.

"It gets to be a real challenge, since nobody, including myself, likes the feeling that someone has outfoxed him," explains Blankenship as he rubs calamine lotion on his fly-bitten arms. "Hell," he adds, "I'd even be satisfied to prove Oak Island the biggest hoax in the world."

This article originally appeared in the Wall Street Journal, *issue of July 27, 1970 and was later reprinted in* Rare Coin Review *No. 8, November 1970, with permission of the copyright owners, Dow Jones & Company.*

The Psychology of Collecting

| By Q. David Bowers | 1985 |

*T*he following article is derived from an interview with Susan
K. Elliott, who discussed collecting ups and downs with Q.
David Bowers and who published the results of the interview in Plate
Collector, *issue of July 1984.*

At the time Susan Knight Elliott was the publisher and editor of The
Plate Collector, *which went to enthusiasts in the field of limited edition art plates. She is the daughter of the late Frank Knight, who at one
time was closely associated with* Coin World.

*While the hobbies of plate collecting and coin collecting are not par-
ticularly alike (except that each involves round objects!), there are certain common philosophies. "What does psychology have to do with
collecting?" Knight asked me. The following text, adapted from the interview, discusses this.*

Susan K. Elliott: Are collectors different from other people?

Q. David Bowers: Yes, I think collectors have a facet of their lives
that is almost like having a private business or a summer home
somewhere. It is an extra section of their lives, an alter ego type of
thing they can retreat into. It adds an extra dimension to their existence. I think there are very, very few collectors who have empty
lives. They can read about what they collect, go to conventions, study,
or have a goal to work on to earn that special item or whatever. I think
this adds a special quality to a collector's life.

Unquestionably, teenagers who are involved in coins, stamps, or
other hobbies stay out of trouble more than do those who have idle
time on their hands. Boredom is not a characteristic of an active collector. Indeed, a typical collector wishes for more time to spend on the

hobby. Also, a collector will always have a circle of friends with a shared interest, a "support group," as they say in psychology.

S.K.E. What has your experience in different collecting areas taught you about similarities between hobbies?

Q.D.B.: The mentality is the same in each. Each hobby has its own rarities, its own prized possessions, Rembrandts or Mona Lisas if you will; each has its objects of desire, its classics. Each hobby also has its common pieces.

A collection becomes an expression of an individual, a reflection of an individual's personality. What you like is manifested in what you collect. In coins, there are no two collections precisely alike. If I were to give 10 numismatists each a check for $1,000 and tell them to put together a group of coins, there would probably be no similarity among those picked out.

I think that one of the nice things about collecting is that it does permit one to be an individual. Our society is becoming increasingly faceless. There is not too much difference between staying in a Hyatt, Marriott, or other hotel in New York City, San Francisco, Los Angeles, or Chicago. All have about the same things on the menu, all reflect a somewhat similar architectural style, and if you were blindfolded and put into a typical hotel room, I defy you to tell me whether you are located in Portland, Maine or Portland, Oregon! A resident of Atlanta can go to Des Moines and have the same McDonalds Quarter Pounder or the same Chicken McNuggets, or in the evening watch the same network television programs. He can buy the same things in the local Sears store, or he can telephone an office of the same stockbroker. It is a plastic society reduced to minor differences among localities and individuals. We have area codes, zip codes, Social Security numbers, taxpayer identification numbers, credit card numbers, and other numbers. Indeed, even the idea of having individual first and last names seems to be in danger! Collecting permits one to have an identity.

Also, the hobbies with which I am familiar offer the pleasing situation that often the most interesting and historically significant things are not the most expensive pieces to own. In the field of old postcards, there are many beautiful subjects which can be bought for several dollars each. In the field of old bottles, many intriguing pieces cost just $5 to $10 or so. To be sure, there are $3,000 postcards and there are $10,000 bottles, but if you had to spend a week on a desert island looking at an item and studying it, the $10,000 bottle isn't necessarily better than the $5 or the $10 one. Similarly, in the field of rare coins, a 1909 V.D.B. cent, an Extremely Fine specimen which costs just a few dollars, is every bit as interesting to contemplate as a Choice Uncirculated 1893-S Morgan dollar which is apt to cost around $100,000. In fact, if I asked you to do some research and prepare a 10-minute talk on either one of these two coins, probably the "lowly" 1909 V.D.B. cent would offer the more interesting presentation! I do not mean to demean the $100,000 1893-S silver dollar, for this is a grand item on its own and is wonderful to possess. I am simply stating that interesting items are not necessarily expensive.

The dealers in various hobbies are similar and share common philosophies of buying and selling. You can visit with a dealer in postcards and then talk with a dealer in coins, and there is not that much difference. I am sure the same is true of limited-edition plates, an area with which I am not familiar.

In all the hobbies in which I have been involved, one can never have true completion. One can never have an example of everything going back into history. Instead, the collector has to specialize in a particular area. By specializing the collector will soon learn more than most dealers know, or even more than so-called "experts" know—simply by applying oneself, reading as much as possible, and learning whenever the opportunity is presented.

In all hobbies of interest to me, I find education is the most beneficial thing. I collect coin-operated nickelodeon pianos. One of my first activities when I began my interest in these many years ago was to lay my hands on each and every book I could find on the subject. The result is that today I have a whole section of my library devoted to the subject. Some are in foreign languages, and I can't read them—but I have consulted them by using translation dictionaries. All are useful one way or another. Similarly, the fields of old postcards and old bottles are interesting to me, and I have fairly definitive libraries in each category.

For my rare coin business, I have acquired books ranging from superbly written volumes to worthless price guides and investment texts that must have taken no more than a weekend to produce. Equally important, I have tried to get every back issue I can find of all the magazines that were published. The subject of magazines and hobby newspapers is generally overlooked. These have a gold mine of information in them, but because they are not bound between hard covers and they are easily tossed away, many collectors do not consider them. However, from a research viewpoint these are fantastic items. Fortunately, some are now available on microfilm and microfiche.

I am sure in your own field, Susan, that of plates, if someone really wanted to become an expert, one of the best things they could do would be to get a file of back copies of *The Plate Collector.* In my personal hobbies and also in my business, books in my library áre far and away my most important asset.

S.K.E.: What factors create a healthy hobby?

Q.D.B.: I believe that healthy hobbies—and I am familiar with such diverse areas as coins, music boxes and other self-playing musical instruments, bottles, old prints and posters, and postcards—all have the same characteristics. A healthy hobby has to have a broad base of people, in my opinion—a base broad enough so there can be organizations and clubs which hold meetings; groups with a special interest. In this way there is interfacing on the personal level and camaraderie. You probably couldn't make a club of collectors of Rembrandt paintings, simply because there are not enough paintings to go around. However, there are enough coins to go around, and coin clubs flourish.

The price structure of the hobby should be *real.* In other words, if a price given to an item is $50 there should be faith in the market value, and someone shouldn't buy a prized item for $50 and find out the next morning that it is only worth $5. There should be a logical basis for buying and selling. There should be some assurance that the hobby, if it involves buying and selling, will eventually result in a store of value being built up. There should be confidence that the classics really are classics and are simply not a twinkle in the eye of a promoter.

The hobby of antique slot machines suffered from problems a few years ago, and so did coins, because many people were buying for the wrong reasons. Purchases were being made for speculation and investment only. Buyers would come to me and say, "I want one of this item, five of that item, and 10 of these." I would ask them, "Do you need these for your collection?" A typical answer would be: "Oh no. I'm not collecting them, for I am not interested in collecting. I am buying them because I think they are going to be worth more next year."

What happens is sooner or later the market runs out of new investors, and the prices come down—which then affects the psychological outlook of everyone.

I think to be healthy a hobby should have a solid price structure, and the buyers should be basically *collectors,* or they should be dealers buying for their inventory. While investing is just great, a buyer should be a hobbyist first and an investor second. In articles and books I have written, including those on the subject of coin investment, I have always emphasized the collecting aspect. Investors buying large amounts of things and putting them away, but without collecting in mind, probably will cause problems in the hobby further down the line.

A healthy hobby should have publications that are interesting to read, well edited, and timely. It should have reference books that are widely circulated and available at reasonable costs. It should comprise a variety of collecting objects ranging from the inexpensive to, perhaps, the rare and seldom-obtainable, although there would be nothing wrong with the hobby in which all items are inexpensive. A hobby should have leaders who are willing to selflessly devote time and energy to the benefit of various organizations and who are liked and respected.

S.K.E.: From your experience, can a formula be devised to predict boom periods versus slumps in a hobby, based upon prevailing interest rates, gold and silver values, or other economic factors?

Q.D.B.: The most important thing so far as boom periods go is psychology. Psychology is the first and foremost factor influencing a boom in any field. Many people come to believe a common thing: prices are going to be higher next year, so they have to buy now. Supplies are limited, and they have to send in their money now, or the music is going to stop and they are not going to find a chair. Boom periods are engendered by a growth in the number of collectors and dealers and by a growth in prices. So, if prices go up and the field is expanding, people say the logical result will be still higher prices in the future. The same people want to buy as much as possible right away.

This situation causes the phenomenon of noncollectors entering the field. In many speculative areas, people who are not involved in these areas all of the sudden want to become investors. For example, around 1974 in Orange County, California, there was a real estate boom. Whenever a new housing development was opened, people would camp on the doorstep of the developer, seeking to buy options not on a single house for their own use but, rather, five, 10, or more houses for investment. Often a lottery had to be held! Prices doubled and tripled within a period of just a few years. This was fine for the developers and for those who got in early, but many later people were left holding the bag—to be more specific, the mortgage! The Holland tulip-bulb mania was an example of people who weren't the slightest bit interested in tulips for their main purpose (as a decorative flower) paying record prices. Of course, that house of cards collapsed and has become a classic in the annals of finance and speculation.

In collecting fields, boom periods are helped along by the entry of new dealers who use flashy advertisements and questionable promotions. In the meantime, established dealers often sit on the sidelines scratching their heads, wondering what is happening. If you were to survey old-time rare coin dealers—say, those who have been in the field for 20 years or more—you would find very few of them ran promotional advertising during the great coin boom of the 1979-1980 years. Rather, most advertising was run by newly sprouted firms with little tradition, background, or knowledge.

Left to their own devices, coin collectors would not generate boom periods. Rather, the growth in collectors and the growth in coin prices would be of a steady nature. There would probably be no sharp rises or sharp increases in the statistics, and then, happily, there would probably be no decreases either. Indeed, such a situation has characterized the coin hobby for most of its existence—punctuated by certain speculative periods such as the commemorative boom of 1935-1936, the interest in Proof sets in 1956-1957, and other cycles, some of which I discuss in my *High Profits from Rare Coin Investment* book.

So far as prevailing interest rates go, if you had asked me this question 10 years ago I would have said high interest rates would dampen the hobby, and low interest rates would see hobby growth. However, during the 1979-1980 era, when coin prices hit unprecedented peaks, at the same time interest rates were unprecedentedly high—so obviously this is not a valid point. When I studied economics as a university student in the late 1950s, the philosophy was the economy could be regulated by manipulating the interest rates—an activity of the Federal Reserve System. However, now all of us are smarter and wiser and know that during the administration of President Jimmy Carter this could not be done. Although the government spends hundreds of millions of dollars trying to figure out what next year's interest rates, housing starts, employment rate, and so on will be, I am not sure their track record is any better than if you or I were to submit our own guesses.

In the field of coins, it is unquestionably true that gold and silver prices, when they are high, spark an interest which spills over into rare coins. Although it is logical that if a gold dollar dated 1875—a major rarity—is worth $15,000 it shouldn't make much difference, if you were to melt it down, whether it would yield $10 or $20 on a metallic value basis; still the value of such a coin is apt to increase if the value of gold bullion goes up. The answer is the popular psychology of crowds. It doesn't make any sense to me.

I feel that hobbies respond to cycles. Hobbies I have studied have often built up to a cyclical peak, and then the cyclical peak has simply run out of growth. I don't like it this way, but this is the way it has happened. In such a peak period, just before a decline, no new clubs are being formed, no new people are subscribing to publications, and no new collectors are being added. All of a sudden there are more shows than anyone can go to, more things on the market than anyone can afford, and a decline sets in.

Prices start shrinking. "This can't be happening!" is the reaction of many newcomers. They get frightened, they become disillusioned, and they say, for example, "Gosh, I didn't know postcard prices—or coin prices—or bottle prices—or slot machine prices—or rare stamp prices—would ever go down, but now that they're going down I'm certainly not going to buy any." Or, "Now that coin prices are going down I'm disgusted with coins. I'm particularly disgusted with coin dealers, who I believed knew in advance this would happen." They might say, "I'm going to leave coins; I'm going to go off and do something else." So, the hobby shrinks, and fewer people invest.

By and large, because of the basic appeal of the hobby, newcomers are brought in. Newcomers find the most interesting pieces to be the most appealing, and they start buying. They find some bargains and realize certain coins—or postcards—or bottles—or whatever—costing $50 a few years ago may cost only $20 today. That's pretty good, they think, and soon you have a new base of collectors, and the cycle starts over again.

In coins I have personally experienced four or five well-defined cycles. Each time there is a cycle there is a different leader in the cycle. At one time modern Proof sets were popular, then in another cycle it was gold coins, in still another cycle it was silver dollars that were the leaders.

To me, this is a somewhat predictable situation. Whenever I see something going up without an expanded base of collectors causing it, the warning flags go up! I say, "Be careful!" This situation is especially true when prices go up unrealistically, things don't seem to make sense to old-timers who have been at the game for many years, and everyone is saying, "Look what that item is bringing now."

S.K.E.: Do you mean predictable in the sense that what is the leader

could have been predicted, or that these normal cycles will occur?

Q.D.B.: If something goes up very slowly and very steadily and is bought mainly by collectors, it will probably be immune to cyclical effects. That is, if you take coins that are classic and basically rare and that aren't in the limelight, those might go up 10% a year, 15% a year, or some other number and they're not particularly susceptible to cycles. In some years they might not go up at all, in other years they might go up, for want of an example, 17%. But, things that go up 25% a year, 50% a year, or some such other price often come down just as quickly.

I should note, however, coin cycles are somewhat like saw teeth. Imagine a saw on its side, slanting upward. Each peak represents a saw tooth and is higher than the previous peak. Each valley is higher than the previous valley. In coins, the long-term trend has been upward, but there have been peaks and valleys. When one is in a valley it is hard to look at the overall picture. Similarly, when one is experiencing a peak, it is hard to remember there are also valleys! Again, we return to psychology. The same thing has been true from time to time in postcards, musical instruments, bottles, slot machines, and other fields with which I am familiar. In March, one of America's leading stamp dealers wrote me a note stating that the stamp market is lousy. If I were in stamps, which I'm not, this would be what they call a "buy signal" in the stock market. As Bernard Baruch has stated, the time to make the greatest profits is to buy when few others have faith in buying, and to sell when others are scrambling to buy. This means swimming against the trend, bucking popular psychology. And, most important of all, it means ignoring the proclamations of various investment experts, who are usually exhorting you to buy whatever they happen to have in stock at a given moment. There is psychology involved, because when you are in the bottom of a cycle, not many people want to buy. As noted, you have to buck the trend. A typical investor might say or think, "Well, I shouldn't buy things now because I'm afraid. Few people reassure me that the items will go up in value. I have to think for myself"—and thinking for oneself is always frightening. People prefer the psychology of crowds, the lemming philosophy.

So, in my opinion, the very best buys are made when the market is low, but it is hard to convince people to buy then. There are very few people who will really study if something is good in the long term. Instead, they much prefer to be crowd followers. In coins, there are many attractive areas at the present time. Colonial coins in many instances sell for much less than they did four or five years ago. I translate this as an opportunity, not as a disadvantage. However, if history repeats itself, more people will want to buy colonials when they are priced five times what they are now, than want to buy them at current attractive levels!

S.K.E. Is it advisable to invest in collectibles for short-term gain?

Q.D.B.: In my opinion, investment in collectibles should only be undertaken in conjunction with a well-reasoned program of *collecting*. I feel if you collect with a basic collecting formula, investment will take care of itself. Your purchases will do well as an investment as long as you are aware of what price to pay and have an eye for quality. An overpriced common junk item is always going to be overpriced. A correctly priced quality item will always be quality and will always be in demand.

I have never been a limited-edition plate collector, but if I were, based on my knowledge of other fields I would probably look at plates as follows:

What is interesting to me personally? What has a basic appeal as to format, or motif, or subject?

How rare is it? If it is common, is it common because a lot were sold due to a large promotion? Or is it common because there truly was a widespread demand on the part of the public?

What is it *really* worth? How does the plate that sells for $100 compare to a plate that sells for $50? Does it seem overpriced or does it seem to be a bargain?

I would ask myself all these things, and then probably I would collect one of each. I wouldn't say, "I want 15 of this and 20 of that." Instead, I'd say "Well, I would like one nice example of each interesting item"—of whatever happened to appeal to me. I know the Bing & Grondahl plates produced in Copenhagen since the 1890s are classics, so perhaps I would at least investigate these. I don't think you can go far wrong collecting or investing in classic items. As long as people collect plates, classics will always be popular, and the same is true with coins and other areas. Prices, of course, may fluctuate from time to time, depending upon the market cycle.

S.K.E.: When hobbies are ranked in order of popularity, coins have long been No. 1. Would you date modern coin collecting from the founding of the American Numismatic Association in 1891?

Q.D.B.: Until about 1933 or 1934, coin collecting was mainly the province of the person who had a den with leather-bound books and who, with the aid of a candle or incandescent lamp, studied books and coins and was a scholar. Then, beginning in 1933 and 1934, coins began to be popular on a widespread basis. Eventually, the Whitman coin folders came out, the *Numismatic Scrapbook* magazine was published, and numismatics became a widespread, popular hobby. Later, the *Guide Book of United States Coins* appeared and helped a lot. So, I would say the modern coin collecting hobby dates from the 1930s.

Truly modern collecting combined with investing started in the 1960s when, all of a sudden, those in the hobby started hearing things like "hard assets," "tangibles," and "collectibles." These were new terms to the field and they date from the 1960s onward. The investment appeal unquestionably has brought in new buyers, some of whom have only been buyers and investors, but some of whom, pleasingly, have gone on to become collectors and specialists.

S.K.E.: That's interesting, because the real growth of plate collecting came in the 1960s when the first collector plate was made in France and went up in value from $25 to $1,700, a situation which brought in many other plate manufacturers. Plate collectors are often told, "Buy what you like, and chances are that the rest of the market will like it too." Those who buy for their own enjoyment are likely to have something that's of wide appeal. Does this contradict your belief collectors should buy based on knowledge rather than emotion?

Q.D.B.: I think that if someone in the field of limited-edition plates comes out with something that looks positively ugly and charge a high price for it, they can send all the fancy brochures they want, saying, "Buy now because it will go up in value," but if it's not basically appealing, why buy it? It has to appeal to the buyer and be interesting aesthetically. It also should have other factors of integrity.

Although I am not familiar with the limited-edition plate field, I suspect rarity has to be a factor. If it is a limited edition, is it truly limited? How well is it finished? I am sure in the plate hobby there are well-done things and poorly-done things. All of these have to be mixed together to determine what is classic and what isn't.

In the field of antique cars, you know, they have certain classics. Rarity, original cost, appearance, social appeal, quality of construction, and other factors contribute to the designation of a classic. The same is true of coins and the same is true of plates, I am sure. Something is not classic just because an advertisement says it is. Something is classic because it has stood the test of time and because it appeals to the aesthetic senses of a wide audience.

In the field of coin collecting, I recommend a collector buy based on emotion. It would be a sorry state if a numismatist were to form a series that did not appeal to him historically, artistically, or aesthetically! At the same time, when it comes to determining what is rare and what isn't, what the price history of the series is, and other factors, there is no question that knowledge plays an important part. So, one should buy on emotion, as you put it, but should temper one's purchases with knowledge.

S.K.E.: Do you think one going into a field as an investor takes a different approach than a collector would?

Q.D.B.: If you go into a field just as an investor you are headed for problems. First of all, if a person goes into a hobby strictly for investment purposes and goes to a dealer and says, "O.K., sell me something," the typical dealer is not going to sell him the hottest items, for those pieces sell themselves anyway. Instead, he is probably going to think to himself, "Aha, what has been sitting on the shelf that I can't get rid of? Let me sell him these, or let me sell him the things I have the biggest profit margin in."

There is no incentive to the dealer, whether he be a plate dealer or a postcard dealer or a coin dealer to say, "Let me sell you the classic, best-selling items that are devilishly difficult for me to find and which I have a hard time keeping in stock." Why should he do that? Those sell themselves! In coins, a dealer might sell things that have been poor investments in the past in order to unload them. They might actually be the worst investments one can imagine. I've seen that happen many times. Time and time again I have had people show me groups of coins saying, for example, "Look, a coin investment counselor sold me this group of pieces for $10,000. What do you think of it?" I'll look at the coins and then say, "Well, these things aren't particularly popular. Why did you buy them?"

"The guy who sold them to me said they were good investments."

"Who is that guy?"

"He was So-and-So Coin Investments out in West Podunk."

"How did you know he had good credentials? Did you check on him?"

"No. I read his advertisements and thought he did. He said he was one of the largest rare coin dealers."

People buy for the wrong reasons. To buy for the right reasons, in my opinion, one should do something like the following—assuming in a hypothetical example one wants to spend a large sum, say $100,000. If a person with such a sum in mind said the following to me, he would probably be bound for success:

"Look, first I am going to spend $500 on books, then I'm going to read them. Then I'm going to spend $1,000 on coins and perhaps later, $3,000 more. Then I will buy some more books. By and large I will spend $100,000, but it might take me five years to do it."

Such a person might well end up with a great collection worth perhaps two or three times the price he paid! However, in the meantime he will have expended a good amount of energy, had a lot of fun, and will have made his own decisions. He will probably do well, but if instead he just threw his money at somebody running big advertisements he would probably lose.

S.K.E.: Where does the market stand right now in coins?

Q.D.B.: We are in a valley following the peak of 1979-1980. Many rarities and desirable pieces are selling for much less than they used to. A lot of investors have left the market because they didn't make the killing they had hoped. Right now there are many good buys to be acquired, in my opinion. Still, there are many poor buys as well. It seems to me it is a very good time to buy coins. It is the valley or opportunity time across the numismatic spectrum.

I have a pet theory that because of the Bicentennial in 1976 and the things that led up to it, the writing of county and local histories, the staging of pageants and celebrations, when all of a sudden collectibles became "pop" items, it became fashionable to collect things. The public built up a great deal of interest, and a lot of this interest wasn't real. People rushed headlong into buying things, whether they were coins or whatever. I think all hobbies experience this to an extent. People were getting into hard items and tangibles, some of them for investment and others for different reasons. This created a faddish element, suggesting that it might be "cute" to collect this, or prestigious to collect that. All of this peaked in the late 1970s across the board—at least in the hobbies I am familiar with.

Now, you have a solid foundation of collectors who are the bedrock of the hobby. This is a good situation. Growth is good also. Speaking of coins, I would like to see a measured growth, perhaps 10% to 15% per year, of price increases in the hobby. This would probably outpace the inflation rate. Anyone who had a nice coin collection would probably achieve investment success.

If I could push a button and say, "I would like the number of coin collectors to double overnight and prices to double overnight," I wouldn't do it, for I think the long-term results would be unfavorable. I would experience pleasures today but would be mortgaging tomorrow. I suspect this also relates to the hobby of plates.

S.K.E.: Would it be fair to say that you think too much emphasis on investment can damage a hobby?

Q.D.B.: I think speculators are fun. They are nice to have, in a way. They provide a sense of the dramatic. Undoubtedly, without speculators things would be rarer than they are. In coins, speculators have saved things. In plates I am sure there are many editions of plates of which 25,000 have been made because 15,000 went to speculators. If they only went to collectors, only 10,000 would have been made, and they would be rarer today. So, speculators in the long run make things more plentiful than they would be otherwise. This has benefits further down the line.

The disadvantage of the speculator is that at the outset prices may be driven up artificially, and if you are not aware of this you may have some problems. I don't think they're necessary to maintain investment activity. I believe that in any hobby if you mind your collecting, then investment will take care of itself naturally and do very well.

In coin collecting, the best investors are those who have built collections. I have yet to see any pure investor outperform any collector. It is like the tortoise and the hare, and the tortoise always wins.

I enjoy reading investment newsletters. They provide comic relief, because it is fun to read, for example, "The insiders are quietly but frantically buying up all the 1946-D Liberty Walking half dollars they can get their hands on." In this hypothetical situation, I can do little but smile, for I know we have 1946-D half dollars in stock, and no one has been asking for them any more than for other half dollars in that era. But, when this "investment tip" appears in print, then the phone starts ringing, and Tom Becker, our senior numismatist, gets requests for hundreds or thousands of pieces! Of course, the person making the recommendation probably "just happens to have" some he might part with to his newsletter readers.

S.K.E.: It has been suggested that emphasis on coins as a get-rich-quick vehicle has given way to a "coins are fun" approach. Would you say this is accurate?

Q.D.B.: I am trying to do my own part to encourage this. There are a number of firms in coins whose basic motive is to service investors, and one of the ways to do this is to say, "You better get in now or you're going to miss the boat." This get-rich-quick aspect will probably always be part of coins, just as it will always be part of real estate or stock. But, I feel the basic market is now a "coins are fun" type of situation or at least it is going in this direction. Right now, many people are buying coins because they enjoy collecting them. That is just great, in my opinion!

S.K.E.: In limited-edition plates we had a tremendous growth in clubs during the peak of 1979-1981 and through the valley that has followed. In 1978 there were about six clubs in the country, and now in the United States and Canada there are more than 140. Perhaps there has not been as much growth in the past year, but during this five-year period there have been many new clubs forming. The clubs are still out there, but buying of plates is not as active as it was a few years ago. Is the pattern the same in coins? Are the collectors still there but just holding back from buying for other reasons?

Q.D.B.: In coins, the number of collectors hasn't changed much, but the number of investors has. As an econometric model, I suggest that there were 100,000 coin collectors in 1977, then at the peak of the market in 1980 there were perhaps 110,000. The actual number of coin collectors did not increase very much. It may have even decreased, because when the market went up to high levels, a lot of collectors got turned off.

At the same time, when the number of collectors went up, from 100,000 to 110,000, the number of investors may have gone from 100,000 to 500,000. So, at the peak of the market you had the 110,000 collectors plus 500,000 investors for a total of 610,000 coin buyers. Since then most of the investors have melted away, thus causing a big price drop, but the number of collectors is basically the same.

The American Numismatic Association, which is mainly comprised of serious collectors, has a current membership of about 35,000. At the peak it had 39,000. So, there has not been that much of a decline.

S.K.E.: How many coin collectors are there?

Q.D.B.: It depends on whom you talk to. The American Numismatic Association has about 35,000 members, as noted. The mailing list of the United States Mint comprises about 2 million people who buy Proof sets and coins each year. *Coin World, Numismatic News, Coins* magazine, *CoinAge,* and *The Numismatist,* the top five publications, probably have a net unduplicated coverage of, I guess, 250,000 names. I estimate that for serious collectors, people who are building advanced collections, most of whom belong to the American

Numismatic Association, there are probably somewhere between 25,000 and 50,000 individuals. Beyond that you have, I would say, 2 or 3 million people, or maybe even more who save Kennedy half dollars or Bicentennial coins in dresser drawers or who may be casually interested in coins but who are not going to subscribe to publications and who don't attend conventions.

Eva Adams, one of the past Mint directors, once estimated there were 8 million people interested in coins. This probably includes some people who simply save current coins for face value. But as far as people who are going to whip out a checkbook and write a check for $100 for a coin because it's rare, you are probably down in the 25,000 to 50,000 range. This is a fine number, by the way, because the number of available coins is not that great. If there were too many collectors, there wouldn't be enough coins around for them to collect!

S.K.E.: Are there predictable types of problems that occur in various hobbies?

Q.D.B.: Yes, one problem relates to false expectations when a buyer expects too much. As president of the American Numismatic Association I see all the complaints that the ANA gets on member-to-member transactions. Many of the complaints have to do with a person buying a coin and expecting that it is in a higher condition than it actually turns out to be. A secondary complaint area involves people thinking items were going to go up in value or thinking that they were going to be rare, but the pieces turned out not to be as hoped for.

Other types of problems involve the financial integrity of different people. The hobby is only as good as the people in it. The dealer community in a hobby should be of unquestioned ethics and good reputation. I know the Professional Numismatists Guild strives to set a high standard, but the human element will always be there and there will always be disputes. This is no different than any other field of human endeavor, I hasten to add.

Education is the answer to most problems. Don't buy anything until you know what you're buying and are familiar with the person from whom you are acquiring it. If a person knows his hobby and wants a certain coin, plate, slot machine, coin-operated piano, and knows how rare it is, what the market history is, what it looks like, and is aware of other factors, he should have no trouble at all.

And, the bottom line is to remember that any hobby should be fun. Enjoy yourself!

From Rare Coin Review No. 56, Summer 1985.

Rainbow's End

By Q. David Bowers   1983

Recently your editor had the occasion to spend the night at a hotel operated by a major chain and located near a busy eastern airport. Early in the morning, before catching a flight to Minneapolis, I ordered a simple meal from room service. Two telephone calls later, following two different explanations of the delay, my tray containing slightly warm eggs and soggy toast (had it been dipped in butter or had it been steamed?—I wasn't sure) arrived. On the tray was a printed notice advertising the hotel chain and stating that "the end of the rainbow is here."

I was pleased to know that by staying in this hotel apparently I had hit upon a real pot of gold. Had I not been so informed, I might have thought otherwise, especially in view of the 30% surcharge notice pasted to the telephone advising me that all long distance calls would be charged by this extra amount, by what I considered to be an uncomfortable bed, by the $95 room rate (not including taxes), by the shoebox dimensions of the room (considering the rate), and by the complete absence of a bellboy anywhere in the area when I checked in.

My thoughts turned to another hotel, this one in Freiburg, Germany, where I stayed a few years ago. Arriving in that Black Forest town late in the evening and without a reservation, I made an inquiry about available hotels and was directed to what at first glance appeared to be a small restaurant. There were rooms for rent upstairs, I was told, and for the German equivalent of about $20 I was shown what I feared would be very spartan accommodations. How wrong I was! The feather bed was worthy of a king's palace, the decorations in the room were hand-picked antiques (not functional modern plastic-covered pressed wood), and the lady in charge told me that if she or any of her family members could help they would be pleased to do so. My bags were delivered to my room before I got there, and my offer of a tip was firmly refused. As if this were not enough, the next morning I was treated, still as part of my $20 room price, to one of the most delicious breakfasts I have ever had!

My airport experience and the sharp contrast with what happened in Freiburg, Germany, prompted me to think about my own coin firm. In today's modern age it is important not to overlook the human element. On the subsequent flight to Minneapolis I resolved that so far as is possible, our firm, despite its attractive sales volume, would never become part of the "big business syndrome." There will always be room, I hope, for personal service of the kind we all like.

From Rare Coin Review *No. 47, April 1983.*

Some Thoughts About Coin Investment

By Q. David Bowers   1970

Recently I had occasion to write an article for *The Fore-caster*, a weekly advisory service. Concluding the article (which was about different ways to sell coins such as direct sale, auction, etc.) I had the following comments:

"I might mention that most leading dealers have their main problem with buying coins and not with selling them. There has always been a good demand for choice material. On the other hand, common material in lesser grades has always been common, will probably always be common, and cannot be expected to be in strong demand by dealers or anyone else.

"Over the years I have seen many fine collections come on the market. Without exception, to my knowledge, anyone who has assembled a choice collection of coins and who has held it for five years or more has made a nice profit upon selling it. While profits are certainly possible in week to week or month to month trading, unless you have the time to keep right on top of the market, it would seem the most consistent profits are made by purchasing choice material and putting it away for a number of years. At least this has been the case in the past. Also to be remembered is the fact that the dealer's margin of profit or sales commission might well eat up any profit made on a short-term basis. However, on a long-term basis this diminishes in importance. . . ."

As a dealer I have seen thousands of collectors enter the coin market, stay for a short while or possibly a long time, and then sell their coins. I have also seen thousands of investors enter the market and achieve varying degrees of success. It has been my experience that, in the long run, the collectors have done the best! To this I attribute the knowledge possessed by the collector. It is very difficult to enter the coin market blindly as an investor and do well without knowing much about what you are buying. By way of analogy, it would be equally difficult to pick winners in the real estate field, for instance, without knowing anything about land use, housing and building trends, population trends, etc. And yet it amazes me how many investors will spend large sums on coins without taking the trouble to even learn basic facts about them.

In the aforementioned *Forecaster* article I noted: "While you are buying coins, or before you buy coins, learn something about them! Persons who have made the most consistent profits have been those who have known the most."

Why Coin Prices Rise and Fall

On page three of *A Guide Book of United States Coins* is a thumbnail sketch of why coin prices fluctuate. Quoting the *Guide Book:*

Prices rise because: 1. The trend of our economy is inflationary. 2. The number of collectors is increasing rapidly, while coin supplies remain stationary. 3. Dealers can procure their stock of coins only from collectors or other dealers who expect a profit over and above what they originally paid.

Prices decline because: 1. Speculators buy and sell in large quantities, drawing in thousands of unwary persons looking for quick profits. 2. Hoards of coins suddenly are released from estates of desceased collectors or Federal Reserve vaults (as in the case of silver dollars) and the like. Such conditions usually adjust themselves within months or a few years.

As might be expected, the coin market is strictly a case of supply and demand. The price of any coin is predicated upon the demand for a single specimen of that coin by a collector who needs it for his collection. Thus the investor who buys a roll of 1949-S dimes has the future of his investment dependent upon the hope that sometime the roll will be broken and the individual pieces dispersed to 50 different collections. The collector, not the investor, is the eventual "consumer." Take away all collectors and coins would be worth face value or bullion value and nothing more.

One of the reasons for the drop in prices in the late 1960s of many United States coins from the highs reached in the mid-1960s was that the "investment market" of that time consisted mainly of investors feeding other investors, with each investor hoping another investor would come along to pay a still higher price. When the number of new investors decreased the demand decreased (bearing in mind the market was made of investor demand, not collector demand) and prices fell. This caused further selling and further price erosion.

What were coin collectors doing in the meantime? They were still collecting. As a result, the prices of numismatic pieces shunned by the average investor remained quite firm. As an example, colonial coins, half cents, and large cents are worth as much today or more than they were in 1965.

As the supply of coins remains fairly constant, any price rise must be attendant upon a rise in demand. Back to my example of 1949-S dimes; there is nothing wrong with 1949-S dimes (or any other later coins existing in roll quantities). In fact, this particular dime is one of the lower mintage issues and will probably be quite valuable some day. But, in the past, the main demand for it has been by investors rather than collectors, so the pieces were not widely dispersed or in strong hands.

Collector demand tends to be steadier than investor demand, so the market for collectors' coins tends to be steadier. The question "Why don't investors buy earlier coins?" is a natural one to ask at this point. The answer is that *knowledge* is needed to collect earlier coins. Also, many investors simply aren't interested in "collecting." My personal advice is for such investors to spend their money elsewhere—the stock market, for instance. It is very, very difficult—here, again, this is strictly my personal opinion—to invest successfully in coins without knowing anything about them.

Disadvantages of Coin Investing

Suppose that you've decided to combine collecting and investing and are embarking on the building of a fine collection with the hope of eventually selling it for a nice profit. What are the disadvantages? Based upon questions I have been asked, here are some that come to mind. Each has an "antidote," and I attempt to give it!

1. Safe storage. Coins are attractive to burglars. Many fine collections have been stolen. How do I protect myself? The answer to this is to keep your coins in a safe place. A bank safe deposit vault provides excellent security at very low cost. A low-amount insurance policy can then be purchased to cover coins in transit or coins kept at your home for study. Take care to keep the coins in a place free from moisture as this has deleterious effects on a coin's surface.

2. Coins don't pay dividends. It costs more to trade in and out of a coin than it does a stock. Yes, it does. If you want a steady income or if you begrudge a dealer his commission, then you belong in the stock market and not in the coin market. But, traditionally, the rewards of coin investment have outpaced those of the stock market. Match the price performance of a random assortment of coins purchased in 1960 and sold today against the Dow Jones Averages and even with the coin dealer's profit the coins come out way ahead.

3. It takes specialized knowledge to invest in coins. Yes, it does. That's what I am mainly trying to say in this article. Would you invest in the stock market by blindly buying the first 10 stocks you heard mentioned on Monday morning? Of course not. Then it doesn't make sense to go out and buy (without checking) the first coins you hear about or see featured as "good investments."

4. Coins are hard to sell. Wrong! In my years of being in business I have never heard of a single CHOICE collection of coins that did not have many eager dealers wanting to buy it! Choice coins and rare coins are always in demand. If your investment "portfolio" is made up of common coins bought at high prices, then I am at a loss to suggest what to do. But, if you've purchased quality you'll have many eager buyers.

Advantages of Coin Investing

As an investment medium coins have much to offer. Here are some of the advantages:

1. Coins are small and easily handled. Even a substantial collection can be easily stored in a small space such as a safe deposit box. Coins can be easily carried from place to place or sent through the mail. This makes the market not a local one, but a worldwide one.

2. Coins are historical, artistic, and interesting to collect. As a hobby, coins combine romance and value. Many fun-filled hours can be spent reading about coins, discussing collecting experiences with others, attributing die varieties, and otherwise enjoying them. Thus, you can combine a fascinating hobby with a worthwhile investment.

3. The coin market is widespread. Hundreds of thousands of numismatists desire choice material. These collectors act independently. This results in an orderly stream of collections being formed and later resold. Spread across hundreds of thousands of collectors, the demand is stable and is not susceptible to widespread sharp fluctuations. As an illustration take, for instance, an 1861 Proof quarter. There were 1,000 coined. To our knowledge, no dealer has more than a few in stock, and most have none. Collectors who have them have just one. Why have two? Thus, they are spread out among many owners. The coin catalogues $140 now. Offer to pay $200 and chances are that you won't be able to buy more than 25 or 50 right away. Dealers who have them in stock will sell them to you, but why should the average collector spoil his set by picking out the 1861 and selling it separately? On the other hand, should you have 50 pieces and try to sell them, there is sufficient demand by many collectors who want an 1861 for their type set or date set to readily absorb such a small quantity. Thus the market in 1861 Proof quarters is stable. As the trend of coin prices moves upward, the 1861 quarter will move up with it. It is a relatively "safe" investment as the demand and supply are both widespread.

4. There is a good demand for quality material. A coin dealer's main problem is buying choice coins, not selling them. If you don't believe this, offer us your collection of choice early United States coins! Build a choice collection and you'll have many eager buyers when the time comes to sell.

Advice to the Investor

Here are some pointers we recommend to the would-be coin investor. Follow them and, in our opinion, you'll do well.

1. Spread your investment among many different coins. If you are investing $5,000 only, then don't buy a $3,000 coin and a $2,000 coin. Or don't buy 100 $30 coins of one date and 100 $20 coins of another date. Rather, buy a variety of different issues.

2. Be prepared to hold your coins for several years. The long-term trend of coin prices is upward. We consider three to five years to be a minimum time to hold them.

3. Don't invest necessary funds. Use discretionary funds or "extra" money for coin investment. If you need funds for day-to-day living expenses, then a savings account would be a better bet. But, if you do have funds for long-term investment in the stock market, real estate, etc., then you might well consider putting a percentage of this into coins.

4. Realize that for your investment to do well, the coin market as a whole must do well. (Now that the stock market is severely depressed, even the bluest of "blue chips" have gone down. Likewise, in a falling coin market even choice coins may remain steady or decrease in value). Don't consider coin investment to be a "sure thing," (is any investment a sure thing?), but to be speculative.

5. Buy coins that have a claim to being scarce or rare. A common coin is common now and will be common in the future. Generally speaking, it is illogical for today's common coin to be tomorrow's rare coin!

6. Learn about coin grading. A polished EF coin bought at a bargain price as "BU" is no bargain. As Lee F. Hewitt, former publisher and owner of *The Numismatic Scrapbook Magazine,* has said many times, "There is no Santa Claus in numismatics." Take, as an example, an Uncirculated 1916-D Mercury dime. A Brilliant Uncirculated one catalogues for $675. We would be happy to pay $500 for a nice one (as would virtually any other leading dealer). So, if you are offered a "BU" specimen for, say, $350, chances are good that it's either: (1) A fake—in which instance it not only is not worth $350, it is worth nothing at all!, or (2) It is an EF or lesser grade coin that has been processed or treated and offered as "BU." The values of coins are well known. Coin grading is important. Know it.

7. Authenticity is important. If you don't know the technical aspects of coin authenticity, do business with one of the many dealers who guarantee the authenticity of what they sell. A fake coin is worthless and is, in fact, illegal to own. Never buy a coin "as is." Note: We might mention that the coin collector and investor is at an advantage inasmuch as there are very few fakes on the market in comparison to the number of genuine coins. Compared to fakes in the art market, for instance, fake coin rarities are few and far between. It's just that fakes are a favorite topic for coin publications. There are two sides to this—and we're not sure which side we're on! One camp advocates that fakes should be widely publicized and played up so everyone takes notice. This undoubtedly scares off many would-be collectors who are afraid to enter the hobby. (This emphasis on fakery is NOT a featured part of publications on art, stamps, antiques, etc.—although the problem exists there to an equal or greater extent than it does in coins.) The other camp advocates that fakes be privately handled without fanfare. This second idea would be more feasible if all dealers would guarantee their merchandise and collectors could be persuaded to buy only from these dealers. But, as no license or even experience is needed to hang up a "coin dealer" sign, perhaps it's best that fakes be nipped in the bud by publicizing them. This is a controversial point.

8. Shop around. Compare prices and quality of several different dealers. Stick with those who give you the best deal. In this way you'll be able to compare grading and pricing and will be in a position to get the best value for your money.

9. Learn about coins. If you plan to spend $1,000 on coins, then subscribe to several different numismatic magazines, join the ANA, start a numismatic library, and learn all you can about coins. There is no substitute for knowledge. Any success we've personally had in the rare coin field we attribute to intense study about the coins we sell. The coin investors who have done the best over the years have been the ones with the most numismatic knowledge. This point isn't even debatable; in my opinion, it's basic.

Conclusions

The ideal way to invest in coins is to form a collection of quality coins in the fields that interest you. In that way you sample the best of both worlds—an enjoyable hobby and a worthwhile investment.

The trend of the American economy is inflationary. Wages are rising and the average citizen has more money to spend. These factors, plus the convenience of collecting and storing coins, make the future of the hobby exceedingly bright.

Investigate before you invest—and then spend your money cautiously and carefully. If you had followed these steps in 1960 you'd have more than doubled your money during the intervening decade. Scarce and rare coins are not expensive, especially when compared to the established prices of rarities in other collecting fields. We think the coin hobby has a good growth period ahead of it. Now is the time to learn about coins—so you'll be at the best possible advantage to participate.

From Rare Coin Review *No. 6, July 1970.*

Buchanan's Silver Mine

| By Mark Twain | 1985 |

My salary was increased to 40 dollars a week. But I seldom drew it. I had plenty of other resources, and what were two broad $20 pieces to a man who had his pockets full of such and a cumbersome abundance of bright half dollars besides? (Paper money has never come into use on the Pacific coast.) Reporting was lucrative, and every man in the town was lavish with his money and his "feet."

The city and all the great mountainside were riddled with mining shafts. There were more mines than miners. True, not 10 of these mines were yielding rock worth hauling to a mill, but everybody said, "Wait 'till the shaft gets down where the ledge comes in solid, and then you will see!" So nobody was discouraged. These were nearly all "wildcat" mines, and wholly worthless, but nobody believed it then. The "Ophir," the "Gould & Curry," the "Mexican," and other great mines on the Comstock Lode in Virginia and Gold Hill were turning out huge piles of rich rock every day, and every man believed that his little wildcat claim was as good as any on the "main lead" and would infallibly be worth a thousand dollars a foot when he "got down where it came in solid." Poor fellow, he was blessedly blind to the fact that he never would see that day.

So the thousand wildcat shafts burrowed deeper and deeper into the earth day by day, and all men were beside themselves with hope and happiness. How they labored, prophesied, exulted! Surely nothing like it was ever seen before since the world began. Every one of these wildcat mines—not mines, but holes in the ground over imaginary mines—was incorporated and had handsomely engraved "stock" and the stock was salable, too. It was bought and sold with a feverish avidity in the boards every day. You could go up on the mountainside, scratch around and find a ledge (there was no lack of them), put up a "notice" with a grandiloquent name in it, start a shaft, get your stock printed, and with nothing whatever to prove that your mine was worth a straw, you could put your stock on the market and sell out for hundreds and even thousands of dollars. To make money, and make it fast, was as easy as it was to eat your dinner. Every man owned "feet" in 50 different wildcat mines and considered his fortune made. Think of a city with not one solitary poor man in it! One would suppose that when month after month went by and still not a wildcat mine (by wildcat I mean, in general terms, *any* claim not located on the mother vein, i.e., the "Comstock") yielded a ton of rock worth crushing, the people would begin to wonder if they were not putting too much faith in their prospective riches; but there was not a thought of such a thing. They burrowed away, bought and sold, and were happy.

New claims were taken up daily, and it was the friendly custom to run straight to the newspaper offices, give the reporter 40 or 50 "feet," and get them to go and examine the mine and publish a notice of it. They did not care a fig what you said about the property so long as you said something. Consequently we generally said a word or two to the effect that the "indications" were good, or that the ledge was "six feet wide," or that the rock "resembled the Comstock" (and so it did—but as a general thing the resemblance was not startling enough to knock you down). If the rock was moderately promising, we followed the custom of the country, used strong adjectives and frothed at the mouth as if a very marvel in silver discoveries had transpired. If the mine was a "developed" one, and had no pay ore to show (and of course it hadn't), we praised the tunnel; and said it was one of the most infatuating tunnels in the land; driveled and driveled about the tunnel till we ran entirely out of ecstasies—but never said a word about the rock. We would squander half a column of adulation on a shaft, or a new wire rope, or a dressed-pine windlass, or a fascinating force pump, and close with a burst of admiration of the "gentlemanly and efficient superintendent" of the mine—but never utter a whisper about the rock. And those people were always pleased, always satisfied. Occasionally we patched up and varnished our reputation for discrimination and stern, undeviating accuracy, by giving some old abandoned claim a blast that ought to have made its dry bones rattle—and then somebody seized it and sell it on the fleeting notoriety thus conferred upon it.

There was *nothing* in the shape of a mining claim that was not salable. We received presents of "feet" every day. If we needed a hundred dollars or so, we sold some; if not, we hoarded it away, satisfied that it would ultimately be worth a thousand dollars a foot. I had a trunk about half full of "stock." When a claim made a stir in the market and went up to a high figure, I searched through my pile to see if I had any of its stock—and generally found it.

The prices rose and fell constantly; but still a fall disturbed us little, because a thousand dollars a foot was our figure, and so we were content to let it fluctuate as much as it pleased 'till it reached it. My pile of stock was not all given to me by people who wished their claims "noticed." At least half of it was given me by persons who had no thought of such a thing, and looked for nothing more than a simple verbal "thank you"; and you were not even obliged by law to furnish that. If you are coming up the street with a couple of baskets of apples in your hands, and you meet a friend, you naturally invite him to take a few. That describes the condition of things in Virginia City in the "flush times." Every man had his pockets full of stock, and it was the actual *custom* of the country to part with small quantities of it to friends without the asking. Very often it was a good idea to close the transaction instantly, when a man offered a stock present to a friend, for if the offer was only good and binding at that moment, and if the price went to a high figure shortly afterward the procrastination was a thing to be regretted. Mr. Stewart (senator, now, from Nevada) one day told me he would give me 20 feet of "Justis" stock if I would walk over to his office. It was worth five or 10 dollars a foot. I asked him to make the offer good for the next day, as I was just going to dinner. He said he would not be in town; so I risked it and took my dinner instead of the stock. Within the week the price went up to 70 dollars and afterward to 150, but nothing could make that man yield. I suppose he sold that stock of mine and placed the guilty proceeds in his own pocket. I met three friends one afternoon, who said they had been buying "Overman" stock at auction at eight dollars a foot. One said if I would come up to his new auction he would give me 15 feet; another said he would add 15; the third said he would do the same. But I was going after an inquest and could not stop. A few weeks afterward they sold all their "Overman" at $600 a foot and generously came around to tell me about it—and also to urge me to accept the next 45 feet of it that people tried to force on me. These are actual facts, and I could make the list a long one and still confine myself strictly to the truth. Many a time friends gave us as much as 25 feet of stock that was selling at $25 a foot, and they thought no more of it than they would of offering a guest a cigar. These were "flush times" indeed! I thought they were going to last always, but somehow I never was much of a prophet.

To show what a wild spirit possessed the mining brain of the community, I will remark that "claims" were actually " located" in excavations for cellars, where the pick had exposed what seemed to be quartz veins—and not cellars in the suburbs, either, but in the very heart of the city; and forthwith stock would be issued and thrown on the market. It was small matter who the cellar belonged to—the "ledge" belonged to the finder, and unless the United States government interfered (inasmuch as the government holds the primary right to mines of the noble metals in Nevada—or at least did then), it was considered to be his privilege to work it. Imagine a stranger staking out a mining claim among the costly shrubbery in your front yard and calmly proceeding to lay waste the ground with pick and shovel and blasting powder! It has been often done in California. In the middle of one of the principal business streets of Virginia City, a man "located" a mining claim and began a shaft on it. He gave me a hundred feet of the stock and I sold it for a fine suit of clothes because I was afraid somebody would fall down the shaft and sue for damages. I owned in another claim that was located in the middle of another street; and to show how absurd people can be, that "East India" stock (as it was called) sold briskly although there was an ancient tunnel running directly under the claim and any man could go into it and see that it did not cut a quartz ledge or anything that remotely resembled one.

One plan of acquiring sudden wealth was to "salt" a wildcat claim and sell out while the excitement was up. The process was simple. The schemer located a worthless ledge, sunk a shaft on it, bought a wagon load of rich "Comstock" ore, dumped a portion of it into the shaft and piled the rest by its side, above ground. Then he showed the property to a simpleton and sold it to him at a high figure. Of course the wagonload of rich ore was all the victim ever got out of his purchase. A most remarkable case of "salting" was that of the "North Ophir." It was claimed that this vein was a remote "extension" of the original "Ophir," a valuable mine on the "Comstock." For a few days everybody was talking about the rich developments in the "North Ophir." It was said that it yielded perfectly pure silver in small, solid lumps. I went to the place with the owners, and found a shaft six or eight feet deep, in the bottom of which was a shattered vein of dull, yellowish, unpromising rock. One would as soon expect to find silver in a grindstone. We got out a pan of the rubbish and washed it in a puddle, and sure enough, among the sediment we found half a dozen black, bullet-looking pellets of unimpeachable "native" silver. Nobody had ever heard of such a thing before; science could not account for such a queer novelty. The stock rose to $65 a foot, and at this figure the world-renowned tragedian, McKean Buchanan, bought a commanding interest and prepared to quit the stage once more—he was always doing that. And then it transpired that the mine had been "salted"—and not in any hackneyed way, either, but in a singularly bold, barefaced, and peculiarly original and outrageous fashion. On one of the lumps of "native" silver was discovered the minted legend, "TED STATES OF," and then it was plainly apparent that the mine had been "salted" with melted half dollars! The lumps thus obtained had been blackened 'till they resembled native silver, and were then mixed with the shattered rock in the bottom of the shaft. It is literally true. Of course the price of the stock at once fell to nothing, and the tragedian was ruined. But for this calamity we might have lost McKean Buchanan from the stage.

The preceding article is taken from Chapter 44 of Mark Twain's 19th-century chronicle of the West, Roughing It. *It was called to our attention by* Rare Coin Review *reader Theodore D. Held. So, Mark Twain, as a "guest author," appeared in* Rare Coin Review *No. 55, Spring 1985.*

Make Mine Moxie!

| By Q. David Bowers | 1983 |

A round 1884 Lt. Moxie, about whom no biographical information has survived today (even his very existence has
been disputed by some), made a particularly fortuitous discovery while
on "military maneuvers" near the equator. The exact nature of this find
was cloaked in secrecy in later years, but students of Moxie-iana, of
which there are many (the author being one) believe it might have
been the herb gentian root.

In any event, Lt. Moxie's serendipity was translated into a commercial product bearing his name, Moxie Nerve Food. This potion, tasting
bitter but with advantages making it worthwhile, was advertised on an
early bottle label:

> Contains not a drop of medicine, poison, stimulant or alcohol.
> But is a simple sugarcane plant grown near the equator and far-
> ther south, was lately accidentally discovered by Lieut. Moxie
> and has proved itself to be the only harmless nerve food known
> that can recover brain and nervous exhaustion; loss of manhood,
> imbecility and helplessness. It has recovered paralysis, softening
> of the brain, locomotor ataxia, and insanity when caused by ner-
> vous exhaustion. It gives a durable solid strength, makes you eat
> voraciously; takes away the tired, sleepy, listless feeling like
> magic, removes fatigue from mental and physical overwork at
> once, will not interfere with action of vegetable medicines.

To a nation desiring recovery of manhood, reduction of imbecility,
and other improvements, Moxie was a godsend. Sold as a fountain syrup and, particularly, in green-tinted bottles, the nostrum achieved wide
sales throughout New England and adjacent states. It was not without

competitors. Ayer's Sarsaparilla, which numismatists will recall was advertised on encased postage stamps earlier (in 1862), had its own following as did Peruana syrup, Kilmer's Swamp Root (made in Binghamton, New York, by a medical doctor who was so successful that from the proceeds he built a large stone building across from the railroad station as well as a brick house, the latter serving today as a community center), Hostetter's Celebrated Stomach Bitters, and other products, not to overlook gadgets and treatments which were not masqueraded as soda pop, Dr. Sanchez' widely-advertised "discovery" of Oxydonor Victory, for example! And then there was a relatively new product from Atlanta, Coca-Cola, which was first formulated in 1886 and which seemed to be claiming a good market share.

Sometime around the turn of the century, Dr. Augustin Thompson, who hailed from Maine but who set up business in Massachusetts and distributed Moxie Nerve Food from there, met up with Frank M. Archer and turned the publicity reins over to him. In Archer he found a genius. Moxie was catapulted from one of many beverages to the forefront as *the* thing to drink. Within a relatively short time the word Moxie was everywhere—painted on the side of buildings in magazine and newspaper advertisements, on lapel pins, on cardboard fans, and even on shirts and umbrellas. All of this was not without its problems, however. The Pure Food and Drug Act, passed in 1906, forced Moxie and its competitors to refrain from health claims. Sufferers of softening of the brain and other maladies would have to turn elsewhere, for Moxie Nerve Food became simply Moxie, the soft drink.

In 1886, the Moxie Bottle Wagon made its appearance. Actually there were over a dozen Moxie Bottle wagons. Most had the same general appearance: a horse-drawn four-wheel cart with a large booth built in the form of an oversize Moxie bottle at the back. From within the booth a uniformed attendant dispensed drinks of the substance for a nickel each. Fourth of July parades, summer afternoons, at the New England seashore, amusement parks, carnivals, old home weeks, and other events and locations saw the Moxie Bottle Wagon doing its thing. As part of the hoopla, aluminum tokens measuring an inch and a quarter in diameter were distributed in large quantities. On the obverse appeared a beautifully engraved depiction of the conveyance, with the inscription THIS IS THE MOXIE BOTTLE WAGON. The man within the bottle, which is marked MOXIE NERVE FOOD, offers a glass to a young boy, while a girl looks on and three adults are in the background.

The reverse of the token consisted only of lettering: GOOD FOR ONE DRINK/MOXIE/AT THE MOXIE BOTTLE WAGON.

How many of these tokens were distributed? The number is not known, but it must have been over 10,000, for examples are seen with some frequency today. Nearly always they show signs of wear, with Very Fine and Extremely Fine being representative grades.

The success of Moxie spawned many imitators. Of the situation the firm noted:

> During the last 40 odd years The Moxie Company and its predecessors have expended much effort and money in introducing Moxie to the public and in establishing its legal rights in its trade mark and trade name Moxie, with the result that millions of people know and like Moxie and it is in demand everywhere.
>
> This is what we have worked for and this confidence and public demand for Moxie has become an asset of tremendous value, the good will of our business.
>
> There is another result, however, of the great demand for Moxie, which seems as inseparable from popularity as shadow is inseparable from sunshine, namely: that unscrupulous manufactuers and dealers sometimes substitute spurious imitations when Moxie is called for, imitate Moxie as closely as they are able in color and taste, and imitate the bottle of Moxie, considered as a package, with its label, shape, color and distinctive appearance. . . .

A California firm came up with Toxie, an imitation, which was successfully challenged by Moxie, with the result that a judgment against Toxie was given in 1914.

In a contest aimed at striking down Proxie, an imitator, Frank Archer testified that more than a million and a half dollars had been spent in advertising Moxie and that "it is sold in almost every state of the Union," somewhat of an exaggeration, at least so far as the geographical territory is concerned. Court proceedings revealed that "Moxie has a slightly bitter taste. It is also apparent that Proxie has a slightly bitter taste," and that the coining of the word Proxie, instead of the regular word proxy (the latter being part of the English language), testified to the intent to confuse the product with Moxie. Rixie, Modox, Non-tox, and Noxie met similar fates. One infringer, Ephraim Provo of Salem, Massachusetts, apparently suffered the indignity and embarrassment of being directed by the court to have his imitation bottles "publicly destroyed." (Wonder how many people watched the event?)

By the 1940s Moxie was on the wane. Coca-Cola had long since achieved domination of the market, Pepsi-Cola, Nehi, Royal Crown, and others became better known than Moxie, Frank Archer passed from the scene, and, soon, Moxie was all but forgotten. Sure, an older generation of New Englanders would never forget it, but school children turned to other things.

All was not lost, however. A few years ago the Moxie trademark was resurrected, and today in certain areas of New England a beverage bearing that name can be purchased.

Moxie memorabilia lives on. For numismatists there are aluminum Moxie tokens showing the Bottle Wagon. For postcard collectors there are views of amusement parks, seaside resorts, and other locations with the Bottle Wagon, or its successor (in 1916) the motorized Moxie Horsemobile (which featured a model of a horse mounted on a car chassis). Old Moxie bottles can be bought in antique shops for a couple of dollars, although the other day the writer saw one with a little white tag marked $4.50. Hand-held cardboard fans picturing pretty girls and the Moxie trademark were made in a number of varieties as were pins and buttons.

From Rare Coin Review *No. 47, April 1983. Later the author wrote a book on the subject,* The Moxie Encyclopedia, *published by the Vestal Press in 1985.*

The 1856 Flying Eagle Cent

| By *Walter Breen* | *1971* |

E ver since the Mint began operations in 1792, copper was the bane of its existence. Expensive and difficult to come by, often available only in hard-to-work forms such as nails or machine parts, or more often still alloyed as brass, copper was a critical raw material both for cent planchets and for gears in the Mint's rolling mills.

By the end of 1795, copper prices had risen high enough so that the Mint lost 22% on its cent coinage; that is, 100 cents cost the Mint $1.22 to make. As a result, on December 17, 1795, George Washington verbally authorized Mint Director Elias Boudinot to begin making lightweight cents at 168 grains apiece. This was a fairly daring step at the time, since copper was considered a precious metal when pure, and lightweight coins were likely to be rejected as worthless. The Mint people cut down off center cents, melted down older blanks and clippings and whatever other copper they could find, and began making blanks at the new weight. Before the end of the year they struck 45,000 more cents (Sheldon variety No. 76b), and in the next few weeks struck several hundred thousand.

President Washington signed a proclamation on January 27, 1796, announcing the weight reduction retroactively, after which the new cents were distributed in quantity.

In the meantime, Mint efforts to obtain copper took stranger forms. Some 32,000 Talbot, Allum & Lee tokens—altogether 1,076 pounds—went directly to the coining department rather than to the melters. They were mostly rolled down to the proper thickness, some being cut into cent blanks, but the great majority into half cent planchets, forming most of the planchets used on the 1795 No Pole variety. At least two large cents today are known on Talbot, Allum & Lee tokens, one of them the Gem Sheldon No. 75 in the Smithsonian Institution; the other the unlisted 1795 discovered by this writer in 1969 and sold, in Fair condition, for $1,100 in one of Lester Merkin's auctions.

Elias Boudinot's major accomplishment during his directorship was negotiating a contract with Boulton & Watt's Soho Mint (Birmingham, England) for copper cent planchets. Purchasing already made planchets allowed the Mint to bypass their rolling mills and cutting presses, and saved time as well as wear and tear. Even with the added cost of shipping the blanks, Boudinot figured the Mint would save money, and would guarantee quality higher than the Mint's own technology could provide. Boulton & Watt was the third factory contacted for the purpose, the others' products being entirely unsatisfactory and more expensive even though domestic. Eventually the Soho Mint got the majority of the Mint's orders. Later on, Revere Copper & Brass and Crocker Bros. & Co. of Taunton, Massachusetts were to surpass the Boulton & Watt output.

Once the problem of planchet supplies was solved, the Mint believed its troubles were over, but they had hardly begun. Banks and merchants seldom called for large cents in trade. Many refused them outright—which they were legally entitled to do, as large cents were never legal tender during their entire period of issue! (They achieved legal tender status, along with the half cent, by the Act of 1864 authorizing the bronze cent and two-cent coins; large cents are legal tender today.)

Underweight foreign copper coins and tokens circulated freely while full-weight large cents were hoarded. Objections to the tokens centered around their manifest lack of bullion value, unredeemability, and so on; objections to large cents mostly stressed their lack of legal tender status, their unwieldy size and weight, and their tendency to become dirty after relatively brief circulation. Many company stores would accept large cents only at a discount; others had the same goods priced differently according to the kind of money used for payment—least for gold, less for silver, much higher prices for shinplasters or copper. Redemption of accumulated cents by banks could not be counted on. And by the 1840s copper prices were again rising enough so that the cost to manufacture cents began to approach face value. By 1851-1853, the 1795 situation had come around again, so that the Mint lost a fraction of a cent on every cent it coined, while their enormous coinages satisfied nobody except the firms supplying the blanks.

Something had to change, and quickly.

At this juncture enter Joseph Wharton, with bright-eyed schemes for getting rich quick by selling the proceeds of his nickel mine monopoly to the United States Mint. Nickel—originally "kupfer-nickel," the "devil's copper," so-called because it was difficult to work with existing machinery and required the fiercest heat to melt—had then almost no commercial use. It was a chemical curiosity almost as unfamiliar as platinum or selenium. As early as 1837, Dr. Lewis Feuchtwanger, an eccentric New York dentist, had proposed the use of "argentan" (one of the varieties of German silver, consisting of copper, nickel, cobalt, iron, arsenic, zinc, and some other elements, often present only as trace impurities) for cents; his altruism in the manner is proved by his offering to supply the Mint with unlimited quantities of the stuff.

The Mint people quickly discovered that no two batches of argentan assayed the same, and used this fact as a conclusive argument against adoption of the Feuchtwanger proposal; but it was not forgotten. Late in 1853, when the Mint's difficulties in procuring copper blanks had reached emergency levels, Mint melter and refiner James C. Booth, one of the foremost chemists of the day, proposed two modified versions of argentan, the lighter-colored consisting of 40% nickel, 40% copper, and 20% zinc; the darker-colored, 30% nickel, 60% copper, which produced an alloy that was slightly magnetic.

All these were eventually rejected as unsatisfactory. Nevertheless, the same alloys were tried again in 1854 on an experimental basis with a Liberty Seated obverse, reason unknown. Argentan and silver were easily confused, a fact which was demonstrated by the coining of a few 1854 half dime Proofs in argentan. They are on slightly broader and thicker planchets than the normal silver ones, and have a plain edge (see Judd No. 166; miscalled "nickel").

Other proportions of copper to nickel were being tried out through 1855, with eight-piece sets of experimental cents being made, comprised of copper, several types of bronze, argentan, and copper-nickel. Many of these had Roman numerals I to VIII scratched into the fields.

Though Joseph Wharton's name was not then being mentioned in Mint correspondence or congressional papers, this man was nevertheless the moving force behind all these experiments. Colonel James Ross Snowden, then director of the Mint, was only one of a half dozen or more highly placed officials who were neighbors and schoolmates of Wharton from the Delaware Water Gap area of Pennsylvania. All knew of his monopoly and of his various pamphlets recommending nickel for worldwide coinage use.

Snowden's historic letter of July 11, 1856, to Treasury Secretary Guthrie, quoted in full by Don Taxay (see *U.S. Mint and Coinage,* pp. 235-7), recommended an alloy of 88% copper, 12% nickel for cents, each to weigh 72 grains. This letter mentioned that Treasury agent Colmesnil was bringing to the Treasury Department some 50 half cents struck on blanks made of the new metal, to show the physical properties. Cents so made would yield an 8% seignorage (face value less bullion cost and manufacturing cost), a figure high enough to benefit the government but not high enough to encourage counterfeiting.

On the following December 4th, Snowden again wrote Secretary Guthrie suggesting that, with official approval, the director should furnish samples of the proposed new cent to every senator and congressman with, presumably, additional samples to go to Treasury officials. These are the original 1856 Flying Eagle cents.

The flying eagle device is a reduction of that made by Christian Gobrecht for the 1836 dollar, mechanically achieved. The reverse wreath was similarly derived from the model James B. Longacre made for the 1854 $3 gold piece. As usual with Longacre's original productions, the relief details were too high, producing difficulties in stacking finished coins, and far greater difficulties in getting the design to strike up properly by a single blow of the coining press.

Most collectors, especially the younger ones, are concerned about the genuineness of alleged 1856 Flying Eagle cents offered them, owing to reported deceptive alterations from 1858 (rarely '57). In actuality, these should be no source of trouble. All digit punches are different; the 1858 date is more widely spaced, being constant on all 40-odd obverse dies of this year, including the overdate. Most collectors use the shape of the 5 as the distinguishing feature; on the 1856 the slanting stroke points into the knob, whereas on the 1858 the slanting stroke points into the field to the left of the knob. The knob itself is differently shaped.

We are now in a position to tell approximately how many 1856 Flying Eagle cents were made and where they went. Rumors, mostly without foundation, have circulated since the 1860s about the mintage, not to mention the whereabouts of most examples. Depending on what you wish to believe, anywhere from a few hundred to nearly 2,000 were made; and from 300 to 1,000 survive in hoards. And so forth.

Letters surviving in the National Archives indicate that of the original mintage, the following were officially dispersed: 21 to Secretary

Guthrie; (February 4, 1857); 62 to the senators of the 31 states then in the Union; 115 or more to the individual congressmen (exact number unstated); two to the Mint Cabinet Collection.

Naturally, the above 485 are exclusive of specimens retained by Snowden and other Mint officials, specimens sent unofficially to collector friends, specimens sent to foreign dignitaries, specimens obtained from the coiner by J.B. Longacre and distributed by him to friends, fellow artists, politcal patrons, and so on. They also exclude several hundred held in stock in the Mint for later distribution to coin collectors, some in Proof sets of the year, others as individual coins. Of course, those intended to go with Proof sets followed the actual manufacture of Proof sets in January; generally, Proof sets for any given early year lacked the copper coins, although these were always available to be added to the sets on the request of each customer. The full number made is still unknown, and the problem is complicated by the existence of anomalous varieties in various metals, some of which, at least, presumed to be restrikes. A fair estimate of the original population would be 800. Many found their way into circulation or became worn as pocket pieces. An unknown number of these are said to have been issued attached to pasteboard cards bearing a description of "The New Nickel Cent."

From Rare Coin Review *No. 11, June-July 1971.*

A Girl Named Zee

By Q. David Bowers   1983

She spelled it with an "s"—or, rather, her parents did when they named her. Elisabeth grew up in Owego, a bustling 19th-century community located on the north bank of the Susquehanna River in Upstate New York, not far from the Pennsylvania border. Like so many other towns in the district, Owego was derived from an Indian name, not much different from the villages of Otsego, Otego, and Oswego, also located in New York state.

Today, Owego is a sleepy river town. An IBM factory on the outskirts, on the road toward Binghamton, lends an air of prosperity, but by and large it seems to the visitor that the main street, paralleling the river, with its Victorian homes and storefronts, must have been busier a century ago than now. Those were the days when John D. Rockefeller attended the local academy, when the statue of a fireman rescuing a child was erected in the town square, and when *East Lynne* and *Uncle Tom's Cabin* drew capacity crowds at the opera house. The John Rogers groups of plaster statuary which decorated many Owego parlors, along with foot-pumped reed organs looking for all the world like miniature castles dripping with carvings, were a century away from the antique shops which would eventually claim them.

Elisabeth's husband-to-be served with a New York company of volunteers in the Civil War. Wounded in Virginia, he was one of the lucky ones who returned. Back in Owego, he worked as a grocer. Sometime around 1870, he met and married Elisabeth. By this time he had gained quite a bit of "book learning," mainly self-taught from reading newspapers and journals. Banking became a new interest, then a new profession, and within a year or two he and Elisabeth moved in to a quaint "cottage"—actually a decent-size house by today's standards—close by the river. The only problem might be flooding during the spring rains, but, as luck would have it, this never happened while they lived there.

In 1875, a daughter, Elizabeth—with a "z"—was born to the couple. Her proud father, who had become interested in saving old coins, sought a few current ones of her birth date. His collection was modest, for he had saved specimens which had come across the counter at the bank. Old half dollars of the 1820s in particular came through the door with regularity. Old copper cents were another interest, and he had most of them, including a well-worn 1793.

For young Elizabeth he had to find something special. And that something special had to be gold. Through his bank he ordered from the Philadelphia Mint five 1875 gold dollars, remitting $6 in a bank draft to cover the anticipated postage and handling. Soon a parcel arrived, and there in a neat little row—all glittering—were five Proof 1875 gold dollars. One was for Elizabeth herself, and when she grew old enough to understand, she would be told that the other four were for any children she might later have.

Elizabeth grew. A pretty little girl turned into a strikingly beautiful young lady who, at the age of 20, gave her hand to an instructor at Cornell College, located in Ithaca, just a few hours away. She moved to the college town, taking with her some furniture—a gift from her parents who, by this time could be called well-to-do—and numerous family mementoes, some photographic portraits, several paintings, and a brass-hinged rosewood box containing, among other treasures, five gold dollars, each bearing the date 1875.

Having no children of their own, the couple traveled widely. Albany and New York City, enjoyable train rides away, became familiar to them. In 1913, they sailed to Europe. On board, a popular subject of conversation was the fate of the *Titanic,* which, not long before, had not quite made its destination along the same route.

In England, France, Germany, Switzerland, Italy, and other stops they enjoyed what in those days was known as the "grand tour"—railway journeys punctuated by stops for several days each at palatial hotels. Friends at home were remembered by letters. Each one was signed "Zee," the nickname, derived from the "z" in her name, by which she had been known ever since she was a little girl. To preserve recollections of Europe, she added to an ever-growing pile of hand-colored postcards to be pasted in a scrapbook upon her return.

Baden-Baden, Interlaken, Monte Carlo, San Remo, Geneva, Rome, and dozens of other places were thus suitably remembered.

The years went on; 1913 faded to 1923, then to 1933, then to several decades later.

Around 1963, a young coin dealer visited Owego to buy some old books. The conversation turned to coins, and the visitor was shown a modest collection of gold pieces which, at the time, the youthful professional numismatist purchased for less than twice face value for $10 and $20 coins, exactly twice face for half eagles, and more for quarter eagles, the going wholesale rate. Alas, there were none of the coveted $1 or $3 denominations.

Pleased with his sale of the gold coins, the dealer in books and antiques asked the young numismatist if he would like to buy five *Proof* 1875 gold dollars.

The answer was an immediate "yes," and the story of Elizabeth was told. The Owego dealer knew her quite well, he said. She was a very old lady, a widow living in a rest home. From time to time she sold him antiques, not because she needed the money but because she wanted to see them go to new owners who would appreciate them. Someday, she affirmed, she would sell the gold dollars, too.

The young coin dealer kept in touch with the Owego bookseller, looking forward to seeing someday and, hopefully, buying the gold dollars which, year by year, kept going up in value. Now, each 1875 gold dollar was a *rarity* in its own right.

The coin dealer moved away—to a distant state. No longer did he visit Owego regularly. Then one day he learned that the bookseller had died. Were there any coins in his estate? The heirs replied in the negative. Did anyone know of an old lady named Elizabeth—she must have died in the 1960s? Again, nothing.

So the story ends. Or has it?

From Rare Coin Review No. 48, June-July 1983.

American Numismatic Mysteries

By Q. David Bowers   1984

How rare is it? How much is it worth? As a rare coin dealer I am probably asked these questions more than any others. The second question, "What is it worth?" is usually easy to answer. For a given Liberty Seated half dollar, Standing Liberty quarter, or Roosevelt dime I can give a rather precise answer. "A comparable 1863 half dollar in our last auction brought $1,350—thus giving you an idea of the worth of yours," might be a typical reply. The numismatic fraternity has many pricing sources to study. The *Guide Book of United States Coins,* which appears yearly, gives an approximate idea of many different issues in many different grades. *Coin World, Numismatic News,* and *The Coin Dealer Newsletter,* published weekly, contain much useful pricing information. *The Numismatist, Coins* Magazine and *CoinAge,* issued monthly, are more article-oriented than filled with pricing data, but still they, too, add to the fund of knowledge. Prices realized in auction sales can be particularly valuable for they tell what someone *actually paid* for a specific coin, not simply an *estimate* of what such a coin *might* sell for. Still, auction prices realized must be taken with a grain of salt. Some prices "realized" actually haven't been realized but, rather, may represent coins that have been bid in by the owner. Other instances may represent deliberate buying at high levels by people having such coins in their possession. I remember watching in amazement in one of our auction sales when a certain commemorative half dollar soared to about four times what I thought it was worth, even by a wild stretch of the imagination. The record price—which it indeed was—was subsequently published in our prices realized and gained mention in one of the numismatic newspapers. Later I found that the two bidders were sent to the sale by a prominent dealer who had several hundred of the coins. The record price in our sale was simply an investment in his own inventory. While there is nothing wrong with this—and while the consignor in our sale undoubtedly did headstands when he saw what his half dollar brought—still it would not be accurate to say that in this particular instance, which happened a few years ago, the price realized was reflective of what similar coins might sell for. Still, on balance, auction records are very valuable.

Pricing isn't much of a mystery in American numismatics. True, few dealers could give you an accurate estimate of certain esoteric patterns, colonial coins, territorial gold pieces, tokens, or other items not often seen, but most can readily spew forth numbers for just about any Mercury dime, Morgan dollar, "type" gold coin, commemorative, or other popular piece you might name.

Still, there are some mysteries among regular American series. Writing in *Coin World* on May 28, 1969, I discussed the interesting situation of an Uncirculated 1845-O Liberty Seated dime which at the time catalogued $80 in the *Guide Book*. I reflected that in a recent auction sale of the R.L. Miles Collection (by Stack's) a piece brought close to $800. I noted: "Among advanced collectors this 10 times-catalogue price will not be shocking. To the slave-to-catalogue type of collector this price will seem preposterous. The answer is that the collector who slavishly follows catalogue values will never own some of these undervalued issues, while the collector who recognizes the rarity of these coins will be rewarded commensurately." By1983, the Uncirculated 1845-O dime was simply noted with a dash, implying great rarity and value, in the *Guide Book,* while a piece in just Extremely Fine condition rated a $700 listing!

Before going on to other American numismatic mysteries besides prices, let me reiterate that there are many *sleepers* among United States coins—pieces which have nominal catalogue values but which really are worth much more. In our auctions of the Garrett Collection (sold for The Johns Hopkins University in 1979-1981) and the Louis Eliasberg Collection of United States Gold Coins (sold in 1982) many pieces brought strong *multiples* of catalogue—with one coin selling for nearly 20 times the indicated listing! As spectacular as such occurrences are—and there were plenty of them in these sales—those "in the know" were not necessarily surprised. The answer is that the catalogue values were too low to begin with.

Recognizing this, it is a practice of certain art auction houses to estimate paintings, statues, and the like on the low side. This is a very clever tactic. Time and time again, as a collector of antiques, I have seen listings done in this manner. I recall seeing a catalogue describing an antique music box, one of my interests. The music box was worth about $15,000—it was a popular and fairly scarce Regina automatic disc-changing model. The catalogue estimate provided by the auction house was around $2,500, if memory serves. Well, you probably already know what I am going to write: the music box sold for close to $15,000, and a subsequent news release noted that those attending the auction were "shocked at the high prices realized" and that the music box sold for nearly six times what it was worth! Presumably, such antics serve to attract consignments from unknowledgeable people.

The same thing occasionally crops up in coin auctions. Sometimes a piece which has not been on the market for years is given a deliberately low estimate so that the sale results will seem "spectacular." A bit more clever (if this is the right word) is the deliberate undergrading of certain coins. Suppose, for example, a given coin is worth $100 in Extremely Fine grade and $1,000 in Uncirculated condition. A piece which is Uncirculated could be described as "Extremely Fine" in the sale catalogue. When the sale occurs, those examining the piece in person during the lot viewing sessions will realize that the coin is indeed worth more than $100 and is indeed finer than Extremely Fine. When the sale takes place, many hands go in the air, and the "Extremely Fine" coin miraculously brings $1,000—or 10 times what it "should." The results: publicity for the truly marvelous prices obtained by the auction house.

My reasons for digressing into these situations is to urge thought and consideration when reviewing price lists, auction results, or other numbers. Still, in keeping with the theme of the present article, pricing information is more easily obtained than certain other types of data.

Rarity can provide other mysteries. That is, the rarity of a coin is often unknown. True, mintage figures are a guide—but only a guide. The rarity may be far different. And, there are different types of rarity. There is the *basic rarity* of a particular variety in all grades, and then there is the *specific rarity* of a coin in a particular grade. I hasten to give a few examples. Of the 1936-D quarter 5,374,000 were minted. The *Guide Book* notes that a VF-20 piece is valued at $14, EF-40 at $30, an MS-63 piece at $285, and an MS-65 coin at $800. On the other hand, the 1936-S quarter, of which 3,828,000 were struck, is valued at $8 in VF-20, $7 in EF-40, $105 in MS-63, and $250 in MS-65. Now, let's discuss rarity:

In worn condition, say VF-20, both pieces are relatively plentiful. In fact, so far as I know, 1936-S is scarcer than 1936-D, catalogue values notwithstanding. Neither piece is particularly difficult to obtain. In Un-circulated condition it is an entirely different matter. Many rolls of 1936-S quarters were saved at the time of issue, with the result that pieces, while not super-plentiful in relation to the widespread demand for them, can be obtained without a great deal of difficulty. The Uncir-culated 1936-D, which by mintage figures alone should be more com-mon, emerges as a *great rarity* in the Washington quarter series. In 1936, when these were released, they were considered to be a "com-mon" issue, and little attention was paid to them. A number of years later it was realized that 1936-D quarters were very difficult to find in top preservation. The supply outran the demand.

So, for the 1936-D quarter you have the instance of a coin which is common in worn condition and rare in Uncirculated condition. Thus, one cannot make a blanket statement such as "a 1936-D quarter is common," or "a 1936-D quarter is rare." It is the condition that makes a coin common or rare.

The situation could be reversed. Take as an example, perhaps facetious, the 1982-D George Washington commemorative half dollar. Virtually all known specimens are in Uncirculated condition. A worn piece in this instance would be a great rarity! Of course, you could rightly ask, "Who cares?"

The rarity of a coin can be affected by many considerations. In general, especially among coins of the present century, the first year of issue of a given type was saved by the public. Thus, a 1909 V.D.B. Lincoln cent, 1913 Buffalo nickel, 1948 Franklin half dollar, 1964 Ken-nedy half dollar and a number of other first year of issue pieces are relatively plentiful, especially in comparison to issues of the same type produced a few years later. Among 19th-century coins the "first year of issue syndrome" is not as evident. For example, so far as I know, 1840 Liberty Seated dollars, the first year of the 1840-1873 design, were not saved in appreciable numbers, nor were 1794 half dollars and dollars, 1839 Liberty Seated half dollars, or any number of other pieces. There were, to be sure, exceptions—and the 1883 Liberty nickel Without CENTS is an example. When these were released it was widely noted that the Mint had made a mistake and would soon be calling these coins back. The Mint never did recall them, but the public thought they were rare and hoarded them in immense numbers.

In addition to hoarding the first year of issue of certain pieces, other coins were hoarded for different reasons. Morgan silver dollars, minted from 1878 onward, were produced in response to political pressure exerted by western mining interests. As a result, hundreds of millions of silver dollars piled up in government vaults—pieces that were not needed for commerce. Years later vast quantities of these were released at face value. In 1962 and 1963 several hundred million silver dollars, most of them Uncirculated, emerged from Treasury vaults to delight numismatists. Interestingly, rather than having the effect of severely depressing prices, in general prices *rose sharply*. This was a result of the law of supply and demand. The supply of Uncirculated silver dollars of many different dates increased sharply, and if nothing else had happened, prices would have dropped like a rock. But, at the same time, the demand increased even more sharply, with the result that today virtually every Morgan silver dollar in the series—with just two or three exceptions—is *sharply* higher in price than it was 20 years ago! When one considers the rarity of a Morgan or Peace silver dollar, the mintage figure plays only a small part in the story. Treasury hoarding, whether or not the pieces were released at the time of issue (some of them were), and how many were a part of the several hundred million that were melted in 1918 under terms of the Pittman Act are even more important considerations.

Hoarding also played a part in the survival of certain American gold coins. In the present writer's *United States Gold Coins: An Illustrated History* book a detailed description of the distribution practices of American gold coins is given. In particular it is noted that most double eagles of the 1920s onward went to foreign banks, where they remained after President Franklin D. Roosevelt recalled gold coins in 1933-1934. Years later these sources, particularly Swiss banks, became important to American collectors, for literally millions of pieces came to light and were brought back to the United States.

"Mysteries" concerning rarity in specific grades usually can be resolved by a bit of study. Methods of distribution, hoarding, mintage, metallic content, and other factors all contribute to varying degrees. Bit by bit the enigmas of condition rarity are being pushed back. David

Akers' excellent books on gold coins have furnished compilations of the auction appearances of various issues in different grades over the years. While stated grades in auction catalogues, particularly those dating before recent times, are often subject to dispute (many coins called "Uncirculated" three or four decades ago would be called Extremely Fine or AU by tighter present-day standards), still the information is valuable on a relative basis. If 40 specimens described as "Uncirculated" appeared of coin A and only 10 comparable-grade pieces of coin B, one can reasonably conclude that coin B in that condition is several times more elusive.

Going beyond the questions "How rare is it?" and "How much is it worth?" many other interesting mysteries develop in American coinage.

In 1873 at the San Francisco Mint 5,000 half dollars *without* arrows at date were coined. And yet no specimens have ever come to light. Why? Were they all melted? Was the mintage report erroneous? The explanation is not known. Melting seems to be a good probability.

Likewise, the 1873-S Liberty Seated silver dollar, minted to the extent of 700 coins, is unknown today. Many years ago Farran Zerbe visited the San Francisco Mint, talked with officials there, and reported to readers of *The Numismatist* that he had new information directly from the Mint concerning the 1873-S standard silver dollars, but so far as the present writer has been able to ascertain, nothing more was ever printed concerning the matter. Again, the pieces may have been melted, or perhaps the 700 coins represented pieces of an earlier issue such as 1872-S.

The coinage of 1884 and 1885 trade dollars is shrouded in mystery. These were apparently obtained from Mint sources by William Idler, a Philadelphia coin dealer. For many years, it has been stated that 10 specimens of the 1884 and five of the 1885 were struck, but just where these figures originated is not known. At one time Edgar H. Adams stated that 264 examples of the 1884 were made, but no expansion of this remark was given. Considering the relatively few which have appeared on the market over the years, 10 seems closer to the truth.

The field of colonial and early American coins abounds with mysteries. Although the design of the 1776 Continental "dollar" can be traced to a $1 Continental currency paper note, no official documentation for the issuance of the piece has ever surfaced. It has been theorized that the exceedingly rare silver impressions (one of which we sold at the Garrett Collection Sale in 1980 for $95,000) may have seen service as a *dollar,* and that the usually seen pewter coins represented some lesser denomination, perhaps even a penny. In an era in which citizens demanded full or nearly full weight and intrinsic value in coinage, it seems highly unlikely that a relatively valueless (from a meltdown viewpoint) pewter dollar would have been readily accepted for that denomination. No one knows much about the origin of the 1783 Nova Constellatio copper pieces, despite the fact that these were widely circulated in the 1780s and, today, are relatively common. The copper coinage of New York is a web of mystery and speculation. While it is reasonably certain that many pieces were struck at Machin's Mills, near present-day Newburgh, New York, still others have been posted as the work of Ephraim Brasher, and/or John Bailey. The precise attribution of the mintage site of certain copper coins of Connecticut, Vermont, New York, and New Jersey is complicated by the hypothesis that certain diecutters such as James Atlee traveled from place to place, perhaps visiting different mints, and by the findings that certain mints, Machin's Mills prominent among them, counterfeited pieces from other states.

The field of territorial and pioneer gold coins likewise has many numismatic mysteries. Where was the Cincinnati Mining & Trading Company located? Did it ever actually engage in the minting of coins for circulation? The same questions can be asked of the Massachusetts & California Company. The field of small-denomination California gold coins is vast and contains hundreds of varieties. These were made in large quantities over a span of about three decades. And yet precious little documentation exists concerning how they were made, who made them, and how they were distributed. Most research in modern times, including the efforts of Lee, Doering, Roe, Breen, and Gillio, has centered on the identification and description of die varieties or on pricing and rarity. Relatively little has ever come to light concerning historical aspects, although the Breen-Gillio text, *California Pioneer Fractional Gold,* has made great strides forward in this regard.

Among regular issue early American coins there are more mysteries than one can shake a stick at. Take, for example, several issues among large cents. The famous 1793 Strawberry leaf cent, of which just four are known, is shrouded in mystery. Why are all of them in relatively low grade?

The famous 1794 Starred Reverse cent, the finest known example of which was described in our offering of the John Adams Collection last year, ranks as one of the most intriguing issues ever produced at the Philadelphia Mint. A circle of 94 minute five-pointed stars is around the reverse. For what purpose? No one knows. It has been variously conjectured that the arrangement was intended as a pattern, that it was "the whim of an idle hour at the Mint" (Dr. William H. Sheldon's thought), or that it was a regular issue struck on a planchet which had raised stars on it (a supposition which does not square with the principles of minting operations). Columns of print have been expended on the 1794 Starred Reverse cent, and in the last century even a poem was written about it! But, still, why it was created remains a mystery.

The 1795 so-called "Jefferson Head" cent is another enigma. Is it a counterfeit? Or, as many scholars now think, was it made outside of the Mint as a sample for a private coinage contact (in an era in which the very existence of the Mint was in doubt, and when Congress on several occasions discussed abolishing it)?

Later cents, too, have their mysteries. Why, for example, were 15, rather than 13 stars put on the obverse of a certain 1817 issue? It could have been a diecutting error, but anyone with a basic knowledge of statistical probability would rush to say that if a 15-star variety occurred, then probably there should be several 14-star errors (for one additional star is a much more likely error than two additional stars), but, yet, no such 14-star pieces exist.

While the present writer enjoys mysterious numismatic items, feeling that an enigma makes a given coin all the more interesting, I know that for many, mysteries are not to be tolerated. Many people prefer that everything be known, down to the last scrap of information, the last adjective, the last decimal point. It is precisely this feeling which has been responsible for the success of many investment books—books which list the mintages of certain coins, give positive statements concerning the rarity of various issues (although in nearly all instances these are simply guesses), and even price projections for the future. Readers old enough to remember 20 years ago will recall that at least two authors achieved success publishing books predicting what Lincoln cents, Buffalo nickels, and other coins would sell for five, 10, or 20 years later. Many of the prices seen in these crystal balls were simply the result of mathematical extrapolation. Thus, if a certain Lincoln cent was worth $10 in 1955 and $20 in 1965, then, obviously, it would double again to $40 in 1975 and $80 in 1985. As a perusal of these publications of 20 years ago will indicate, very few predictions came true. But the predictions certainly helped sell books.

Price projections, of course, come with varying degrees of expertise behind them. Sometimes well-known authors and students have made projections. As an example, Anthony Swiatek suggests in the Breen-Swiatek book, *The Encyclopedia of United States Silver and Gold Commemorative Coins,* that an MS-65 Albany half dollar may be worth over $1,200 by 1985, and that two years from now the Bridgeport Centennial half dollar may be worth more than $950—and we hope it will be. By the way, as a dealer we *appreciate* these various projections, for they certainly are an aid to our own business. Nothing helps sell a $500 coin more than having a client read someplace else that it's going to be worth $1,000, $2,000, or whatever a few years from now!

The same desire for precision has made it frustrating for collectors, particularly those who have recently entered the field, when they realize that grading is an art as well as a science. Thus, while a grade such as "Choice Uncirculated" might not sound very precise, and might almost sound like an opinion (which it is), somehow a number such as MS-65 sounds mathematically accurate. MS-65, it could be thought, represents a coin which is better than MS-64.9 but not quite as good as a coin which is MS-65.1! Of course, we are being facetious at this point, but it serves to illustrate the idea.

Come to think of it, it would not be much fun if everything were known. The so-called "mystery of life" is what makes our very existence interesting! I, for one, would not want to know precisely what I will be doing next year at this time, what new friends I will have met, or for that matter, precisely what certain coins will be selling for. Perhaps you feel the same!

From Rare Coin Review *No. 50, January-March 1984.*

Outstanding American Coin Hoards

| By Bruce Lorich | 1978 |

Many collectors have heard—over and over again—such names as the Nichols Hoard and the Randall Hoard without knowing many of the actual details about them, so I thought it would be worthwhile to recount the known facts about some of our most famous coin finds. I say "known facts" because, in most cases, the published information is scanty.

Let's start with what are perhaps the two most famous—or at least the largest—of all coin hoards discovered in the United States. The first, which also happens to be the largest hoard of gold ever found, is known as the Baltimore Gold Hoard. Back in August 1934, two teenage boys were rooting around in the dirt cellar of an old, abandoned house in Baltimore, Maryland. They discovered—hold your hat!—some 3,600 gold coins minted before the Civil War, and probably hidden since that dread encounter. These coins were probably squirrelled away by a wealthy citizen who feared that Confederate soldiers might invade Baltimore and make a house-to-house search for riches (as was done by British troops during the Revolutionary War in Philadelphia and other towns). A tale of woe probably lies behind this hoard—because, for some unknown reason, this gentleman of Baltimore never returned to unearth his fortune in gold. When the two boys discovered the hoard in 1934, relatives of the house's former owners took the boys to court to prevent them from holding onto the coins, but the court recognized the principle of "finders, keepers" and awarded all of the money to the two lucky young men!

This fortune was auctioned to collectors in 1935, netting the boys more than $19,500 (the face value was some $11,400). Amazingly enough, then, the two fellows returned to the cellar of that old house and dug up an additional $8,000 to $10,000 face value in gold coins—despite the fact that dozens of other treasure hunters had hacked wildly at the cellar's floors and walls looking for the same thing. Evidently luck played more than a small role in the treasure hunters' success.

The total face value of the Baltimore Gold Hoard came to just a little over $20,000—a huge sum during that Depression year. Gold coins from the mints at Philadelphia, New Orleans, Charlotte, Dahlonega, and San Francisco were involved: 317 double eagles, 83 eagles, 256 half eagles, 66 quarter eagles, and a whopping 2,903 $1 gold pieces! And this was just the contents of the first of the two finds (the only part of which we have a detailed record).

The best piece in the hoard was an 1856-O double eagle, described as "Very Fine" (a grade which, during the 1930s, meant anything from Extremely Fine to Mint State with toning). It sold for $105, a lot of cash then but nothing compared to today's value of more than $30,000.

The second of the two really famous American coin hoards is my all-time favorite—the Economite Treasure. This was a gigantic cache of silver coins, mostly American, which came to light in 1878 after years underground.

Again the fearsome Civil War figured in the story. The notorious rebel, General John H.Morgan, leader of Morgan's Raiders, struck a great deal of terror in the hearts of northerners living close to the Mason-Dixon Line. He had accomplished a number of what amounted to terrorist attacks on towns just slightly north of the border during the early years of the Civil War. In July of 1863 his boldest exploit unfolded—a raid which brought about his own end.

Commanding several thousand Confederate troops, Morgan crossed the Ohio River and started plundering and burning hamlets and towns. He managed to elude a Union force of 10,000 troops sent out to stop him, then captured a northern steamboat and sailed east along the river until he reached the eastern boundary of Ohio, apparently planning to raid western Pennsylvania next. Unfortunately for him, a huge Union force ended his series of guerrilla victories, reducing his army to 300 desperate men and capturing Morgan himself. It ended his reign of terror and bloodshed, but not our story.

Just 18 miles from Pittsburgh, Pennsylvania, near where Morgan was captured, lay the peaceful community of Economy, a settlement of several hundred religious and social zealots founded in 1825 by George Rapp, who had emigrated to America (as had so many) in 1803 to escape religious persecution in Europe.

Rapp first established the famous settlement of Harmony along the Wabash River in Indiana in 1815. After 10 years he sold this site to Robert Owen, the famous socialist, for $150,000 cash—moving his followers to Economy in 1825, which they purchased with about half of the money received for Harmony.

Now here's where the story gets fascinating. Fearing a potentially bloody raid by General Morgan, the Rappites hid a great sum of money beneath one of their buildings, and apparently lived in such dread of the war and horrible Reconstruction days which followed it that they left their money buried until late in the 1870s, when about $75,000 in silver coins were retrieved from the ground. It was very likely the remainder of the $150,000 which they had received in payment for Harmony back in 1825—for all the coins were dated before that year.

An accounting, of sorts, was made of this loot when it was listed in a coin auction catalogue (issued by Capt. John Haseltine) published in 1885. There was also a list made by a cashier of the bank handling the sale of the hoard. Itchy to learn what the hoard contained? Well, swallow hard! There were 117,000 half dollars dated before 1837—including more than 111,000 Bust halves, 150 dated 1794, 3,500 dated 1805 and 1806, and even two 1796 and one 1797 piece (though—most ironically—these three rarest pieces were spent for their face value before anyone decided to contact coin collectors).

There were also 3,708 silver dollars made before 1804—a single 1794, 800 1795s, and 1,262 1799s. In fact, every date from 1794 to 1803 was included in the unearthed treasure. Bespeaking their relative rarity, only 400 quarter dollars were found, all dated from 1818 to 1828. And silver coins from South America and Europe (which were basic to our circulating money in the first half of the 19th century) totaled some $12,600 face value in the Economite Treasure—which must still be regarded as one of the greatest sources of coins for the American collector.

Not so remarkable as those two hoards, but important nonetheless, are a number of other hoards located on American soil. Let's review them briefly.

The Goodhue-Nichols Find (most commonly known today as the

Nichols Hoard) consisted of a bag of large cents, all dated 1796 and 1797. These were dispersed during the late 1850s, having been bought at the Mint in 1797. Goodhue was the name of the original purchaser, and Major C.P. Nichols apparently inherited the bag. The hoard was kept in either Massachusetts or Pennsylvania—and the cents probably sold for about a dollar apiece.

It's interesting that the bag of cents, direct from the Mint, contained coins of two different dates—and the cents can be identified today because they were on very high-quality planchets supplied by the English firm of Boulton & Watt (the Soho Mint of Birmingham). About 1,000 coins were in the bag when it was broken up, and today most Mint State 1796 and 1797 cents may be pretty safely described as having come from this hoard.

Many pre-Revolutionary War coins, which can no longer trace their sources, probably came from the largest hoard of colonial Massachusetts silver coins ever located. This was the Roxbury Find, named for Roxbury, Massachussetts, where a little boy reportedly discovered a number of practically Mint State Oak Tree and Pine Tree silver shillings, sixpences, threepences, and twopences. This sparsely described hoard came to light in 1863 and was sold piece by piece by W. Elliot Woodward, well-known coin dealer of his day.

The Randall Hoard is another of the really famous coin hoards of the last century. Most Mint State cents dated 1816, 1817, 1818, 1819, and 1820 must have come from this find. Our imagination is stirred when we recall that at least one full keg (and possibly more) of Mint State cents was found beneath a railroad station in Georgia shortly after the Civil War ended. When you figure that a keg at that time contained about 14,000 cents, you know what a fabulous hoard we're discussing!

The hoard is named after John Swan Randall, a collector from New York state who purchased the keg practically intact. The keg's finders had sold the coins, in the original Mint keg, to a drygoods firm in New York, who had thought to use them as a promotional gimmick—they thought it would be memorable if they passed them out as change to customers, for large cents had disappeared from circulation, and these were all bright and shiny. The public, though, suspected them as counterfeits and refused to accept the "big pennies," causing the firm (William H. Chapman & Co.) to cease distributing them. At this time Randall, a serious collector, learned about the hoard and went to the store to purchase them. All but a few were in the hoard when it came into Randall's hands—and he paid just 90 cents per 100 to buy them!

Most of the Randall Hoard cents seem to have been dated 1818 and 1820, with reports indicating that some coins dated 1825 may also have been part of this wonderful find. A natural question to ask is—why a variety of dates in a Mint-issued keg? The answer is simple: the Philadelphia Mint produced many cents before the Civil War, for these were the equivalent to the dollar today, the basic piece of money. Coins would accumulate from various years, and at times the Mint would keg these leftovers, store them, and ship them when requested. That must have been how the Randall Hoard came to arrive in Georgia, but how they managed to get buried under a railroad platform will probably remain a mystery forever.

A hoard of Mint State colonial coins? This sounds impossible, but the seasoned numismatist knows that nothing is impossible when it comes to the existence of coins. The Bank of New York Hoard was—believe it or not—a keg of Fugio cents, all of them Uncirculated! This New York City bank was founded in 1784 and may well have acquired these fascinating coins of the colonial period (actually minted just after the United States formally came into existence) for use as change at the time. Strangely enough, it is thought that this hoard has not been entirely dispersed, even today.

Another hoard of coins from the late colonial period is well known—Colonel Cohen's Virginia halfpenny find. It is the principal (and perhaps only important) source of Mint State examples of these interesting coins.

This hoard dates to the 1870s (a period which is common to most of the important American coin finds), when Colonel Mendes I. Cohen (a ranking officer from the War of 1812 and the Mexican War in the 1840s) somehow got ahold of a large original group of halfpennies minted for use in Virginia. The Colonel was an apparently tireless antiquarian, and coins were just one of his many interests. Anyway, he and his heirs accomplished a slow and well-planned distribution of the coins, in order to uphold their market value. This procedure went on for some years until, in 1929, the final group of about 2,200 of these coins was sold at once in an auction in Baltimore. This blunt method of selling coins which are genuinely valuable and of historic importance drove the price at the time down to a few cents apiece and confirmed that this much-rumored hoard did indeed exist. Unfortunately, the final sale was for strictly commercial reasons, and no solid information about the source of the hoard or the total number of coins originally in it was disclosed. But then this is what makes coin hoards all the more fascinating!

Small groups of double eagles and other United States gold coins have regularly shown up in ghost towns and the like, so the Hull, Texas Find reported in *The Numismatist* in 1937 doesn't appear to be anything much out of the ordinary, except for one brief mention. It included an 1861-S coin which wasn't of the usual design, exactly—but at that time the rare Paquet reverse was not so well known as it is today. This is the only Paquet double eagle I've ever heard of being discovered in an American hoard, so it seems particularly notable. I like handling this rarity and would really like to have seen this one, for its circumstances fascinate me. The presence of this single Paquet piece in an otherwise insignificant hoard in Texas demonstrates two things of importance to the coin collector: how widely West Coast minted gold circulated, and the strange habit rarities have of eluding commercial interests (such as melters) and numismatists—only to pop up in the most unexpected places!

I've kept another really gigantic hoard until nearly last because of its distinctive nature. The Aaron White Hoard was a hoard in the true meaning of the word—the indiscriminate accumulation of a miser. But it tells us a lot about the coins in circulation just before the Civil War.

Aaron White was an attorney practicing in Connecticut at the outbreak of the war, and he must have become convinced of the need to save money for his own survival, in case the North should lose the war—because he gathered only small, readily spendable coins. It seems that he converted all of his paper currency into coins of low face value—every one he could get hold of. It has been suggested that this action did not make sense, since any fearful citizen would have hoarded silver and gold for their intrinsic worth. But, in view of White's hoard, it must be supposed that he hoped the war would be won by the Union and small coins would be most useful in purchasing needed goods afterwards—and, in the bargain, would be valuable if greenbacks failed to hold their value. Aaron White was evidently a very practical man!

Fortunately the war ended with the United States intact, but unfortunately Aaron White did not live to use up his gigantic accumulation of coins. Sold at auction in 1888 (Frossard's 85th sale, held July 20) and privately to collectors after his death—pretty much at their face value—were some 60,000 large cents (most in fairly low grades), another 60,000 copper-nickel cents (most of which White had purchased directly from the Mint but preserved poorly), about 5,000 two-cent pieces, as many as 30,000 foreign copper coins (countries unknown), more than 1,700 tokens (brass, copper, and white metal—many of them Civil War tokens), and between 200 and 300 colonials—coins from early Connecticut, New Jersey, Massachusetts, Vermont, and the other eastern seacoast colonies. All of these latter coins were coppers minted in the 1700s. There were also nearly 1,000 half cents made after 1800.

The Aaron White Hoard is of greatest importance to numismatists because, in its own unintended way, it discloses the kinds of coins which were to be found in circulation up until the Civil War. It also proves the old argument many of America's early coins had not been melted during the first decades of the Republic but been saved, in large quantities in the populated parts of the country, perhaps for sentimental reasons—only to be parted with when money was so desperately needed, when the Union seemed on the verge of breaking up.

The final hoard to be discussed here is, in some ways, the most remarkable of the lot. It is known as the Thayer County Find—and consisted of a bag of 58 territorial gold coins minted by the California firm of Kellogg & Co. Again, it was two boys whose luck drew them to this fabulous find.

The year was probably 1908, and the place was the outskirts of a town in Nebraska. The coins were all of the $20 denomination—and imagine their eyes when those two little boys opened an old bag and out tumbled these bulky gold pieces! How did California gold happen to reach a wooded spot in Nebraska? The probable answer (for, again, the truth was not found along with the coins) is that two ranchers were murdered by Indians while Nebraska was still an Indian territory, and their gold was lost. The scene of the tragedy was like something out of a Western movie: the ranchers made it to a cave, where they held off the Indians with a blockade of trees and underbrush at the mouth of the cave, but the Indians set fire to this "fortification" and burned out the ranchers. Their charred bodies were later found by an Army troop but their fortune in gold was not discovered until many years later—when the two little boys found that bag of Kellogg double eagles in the woods not far from the cave. Was the golden hoard hastily hidden in the brush when the ranchers saw the warlike Indians approaching, or was it perhaps flung from the cave in a desperate effort by the ranchers to keep their gold—at all costs—from falling into the wrong hands?

We'll never know—but that's what makes coin hoards one of the neatest aspects of numismatics, isn't it?

From Rare Coin Review *No. 30, 1978 Silver Anniversary Edition.*

Humor and Notes

By Q. David Bowers — 1984

A great many catalogues offer for sale interesting coins and other items from the late 19th and 20th centuries. What was American life like then? Of course, this is a broad question, and there is no quick answer. What was American humor like then? A reflection of the humor of the times—also observations on other subjects—is to be found among the many almanacs issued by various companies and individuals. Believing some of these notes from years ago might be interesting to our readers today, we looked through some copies of Hostetter's Almanac and Ayer's American Almanac and noted some things that caught our fancy. We share them with you:

WHAT is the difference between a hungry man and a glutton? Answer: One longs to eat, and the other eats too long!—*Hostetter's Almanac, 1871.*

A YANKEE who had never paid more than 25 cents to see an exhibition went to a New York theatre one night to see the *Forty Thieves.* The ticket-seller charged him 75 cents for a ticket. Passing the ticket back, he quietly remarked: "Keep it mister, I don't want to see the other 39," and out he walked.—*Hostetter's Almanac, 1882.*

A WALL between two preserves friendship.—*Ayer's Almanac, 1871.*

A WIDOW who was weeping over the new-made grave of her husband, finally dried her eyes and said, "There's one comfort in it, anyhow; I shall know where he is at night."—*Hostetter's Almanac, 1882.*

OLD BOYS have their playthings as well as young ones; the difference is only in the price.—*Ayer's Almanac, 1872.*

IT PAYS BETTER not to do a wrong than to do it and then repent.—*Hostetter's Almanac, 1883.*

WHY is a wife like a bad bill? Because she is difficult to get changed.—*Hostetter's Almanac, 1873.*

CARPETS are purchased by the yard but worn by the foot.—*Ayer's Almanac, 1870.*

GENIUS. Alexander Hamilton once said to an intimate friend: "Men give me some credit for genius. All the genius I have is just this—when I have a subject on hand I study it profoundly. Day and night it is before me. I explore it in all its bearings. My mind becomes pervaded with it. Then the effort which I make is what the people call the fruit of genius. It is the fruit of *labor* and *thought.*"—*Hostetter's Almanac, 1884.*

WHAT STATE is high in the middle and round at both ends? O-hi-o.—*Ayer's Almanac, 1869.*

NEWS COMMENT: Dr. Hayes wishes to go north again. No arctic explorer is really happy until he has failed to come back.—*Ayer's Almanac, 1871.*

"JUST MY LUCK," moaned a Philadelphia man, "here I've been paying heavy premiums on a life insurance policy for 20 years, and I'm not dead yet."—*Hostetter's Almanac, 1886.*

WHAT WORD of five letters can lose two and still have ten left? Often.—*Ayer's Almanac, 1871.*

A YOUTH was endeavoring to enjoy an evening in the company of a young lady upon whom he had called, but found a serious obstacle in the person of a stern father, who at length ventured very plainly that the hour for retiring had arrived. "I think you are correct, my dear sir," returned the unabashed young man, "we've been waiting for you to go to bed for over an hour."—*Hostetter's Almanac, 1884.*

LOVERS, like armies, get along well enough until they are engaged.—*Ayer's Almanac, 1969.*

PUTTING THE FEET in hot water will invariably cure a headache, from whatever cause it arises. The head aches when, from any cause, the little blood vessels in the brain are too full. Putting the feet in hot water draws the blood from the head.—*Hostetter's Almamac, 1900.*

"THIS DINNER is not fit for a hog!" To which the mistress of the house replied: "How do you know? Have you tried it?"—*Ayer's Almanac, 1863.*

IT IS EASY TO LOVE your neighbor as yourself if your neighbor happens to be a pretty girl.—*Hostetter's Almanac, 1896.*

IMITATION is the homage stupidity pays to genius.—*Ayer's Almanac, 1863.*

AN ARAB died, leaving 17 camels. He willed one-half to his eldest son, one-third to the second, and one-ninth to the third son. While disputing about the division, a camel driver came along and offered to settle the question. This he did by loaning them one of his own camels, thus making 18 in all, then the division was easy. No. 1 took nine camels, No. 2 six camels, and No. 3 two camels—17 in all—and the borrowed camel was then restored to its owner. How can we explain the fact that each son got his share and something over?—*Hostetter's Almanac, 1898.*

WHY is the wayward locomotive so easily controlled by a switch? Because it has a tender behind.—*Ayer's Almanac, 1869.*

THE UNITED STATES gold dollar contains 25.8 troy grains. The ordinary pound, avoirdupois, contains 7,000 grains, therefore $1,000,000 in gold coin weighs 3,686.4 pounds avoirdupois, or over a ton and a half. The standard silver dollar weighs 412.5 grains, and $1,000,000 in the United States silver coinage will weigh 56,931 pounds, or nearly 28 and a quarter tons.—*Hostetter's Almanac, 1897.*

A MAN with an inveterate habit of talking to himself, when asked why, said he had two reasons: One, "He liked to talk to a sensible man;" the other, "He liked to hear a sensible man talk."—*Ayer's Almanac, 1861.*

A LIAR is tolerated when he tells what we wish to believe.—*Ayer's Almanac, 1873.*

THE LAMB and the lion may lie down together, but the lion will be the only one to get up.—*Hostetter's Almanac, 1899.*

JEFFERSON'S 10 RULES FOR SUCCESS: Never put off 'till tomorrow what you can do today. Never trouble another for what you can do yourself. Never spend your money before you have it. Never buy what you don't want because it is cheap. Pride costs more than hunger, thirst, and cold. We seldom repent of having eaten too little. Nothing is troublesome that we do willingly. How much pain the evils have cost us that have never happened. Take things always by the smooth handle. When angry count to 10 before you speak; if very angry, count to 100.—*Ayer's Almanac, 1877.*

DEW is a great respecter of colors. To prove this take pieces of glass or boards and paint them red, yellow, green, and black. Expose them at night and you will find that the yellow will be covered with moisture, that the green will be damp, but the red and the black will be perfectly dry.—*Hostetter's Almanac, 1865.*

WHAT do young ladies look for in church? The hims.—*Ayer's*

Almanac, 1861.

WHEN a clock strikes, it is working; but when a man strikes, he isn't.—*Hostetter's Almanac, 1895.*

THE LOCUST can be heard one-sixteenth of a mile. An ordinary man will outweigh 15,000 of them. Were his voice proportional to his weight, in the ratio of the locust's, he would be heard over 1,000 miles! A flea weighs less than a grain, and leaps a yard and a half. Were a man of 150 pounds weight possessed of equivalent agility, he could spring from the dome of the Capitol building in Washington to China and almost go around the world in two jumps.—*Ayer's Almanac, 1874.*

GOD and the doctor we alike adore
When on the brink of danger, not before;
The danger past, both are like requited;
God is forgotten and the doctor slighted.
   —*Hostetter's Almanac, 1889.*

"AH! Jimmy, you're too late; you did not run fast enough." "Yes I did," said Jimmy, "but I didn't start soon enough!"—*Ayer's Almanac, 1874.*

THE LAST JOKE at the expense of the French Society for the Protection of Animals is to the following effect: a countryman, armed with an immense club, presents himself before the president of the society and claims the first prize. He is then asked to describe the act of humanity on which he founds his claim. "I saved the life of a wolf," replied the countryman, "I might easily have killed him with this bludgeon," and he swings his weapon in the air, to the intense discomfort of the president. "But where was the wolf?" inquired the latter, "what had he done to you?" "He had just devoured my wife," was the reply. The president reflected an instant and then said, "My friend, I'm of the opinion that you have already been sufficiently rewarded."—*Hostetter's Almanac, 1877.*

A WORTHY QUAKER wrote thus: "I expect to pass through this world but once. If, therefore, there be any kindness I can show, or any good thing I could do to any fellow human being, let me do it now. Let me not defer or neglect it, for I will not pass this way again."—*Hostetter's Almanac, 1884.*

A BANK NOTE is better than hard money, because if you fold it, you find it in-creases.—*Ayer's Almanac, 1871.*

DID ANY GET AWAY? The *Indianapolis Sentinel* tells a rich joke of a railroad conductor who resides in that city. In his absence his wife presented him with a fine boy. Some of his wife's friends, who are of a waggish turn of mind, suggested that they borrow two other babies in the neighborhood, and present the three youngsters to their happy father on his return. The plan was carried out, and upon the arrival of the train in the evening, the young husband, who had heard that all was well, hurried home. After fondly kissing his wife, he asked to see the little stranger. Imagine his surprise on beholding three babies when the coverlet was turned down. After gazing in profound astonishment for several minutes, he turned to his wife and cooly asked, "Did any get away?"—*Hostetter's Almanac, 1871.*

A YOUNG WIDOW, who raised a magnificent monument over her late husband, inscribed upon it, "My grief is too great for me to bear." After her marriage to a second husband, upon her attention being called to the inscription, she amended it by adding the word "alone."—*Hostetter's Almanac, 1898.*

THE GRAND ESSENTIALS of happiness in this life are: something to do, something to hope for, and something to love.—*Ayer's Almanac, 1863.*

IN 1813 postage rates in the United States were: single letters by land, 40 miles, 8c; 90 miles, 10c; 150 miles, 12½c; 300 miles, 17c; 500 miles, 20c; over 500 miles, 25c. Double letters, twice the single rates, one ounce at the rate of four single letters.—*Hostetter's Almanac, 1898.*

"THE FIRST STEP towards wealth," it has been said, "is the choice of a good wife." "And the first step toward securing a good wife is the possession of good wealth," says another. Here we have one of those good rules which works well both ways.—*Hostetter's Almanac, 1881.*

JENKINS told his son, who proposed to buy a cow in partnership, to be sure to buy the hinder half, as it eats nothing and gives all the milk.—*Ayer's Almanac, 1873.*

HORACE GREELEY used to tell this story: He once sent a claim for collection to a western lawyer, and regarding it as a rather desperate claim, told the attorney if he collected it he might reserve half the amount for his fee. In due time Greeley received the following letter: "Dear Sir—I have succeeded in collecting my half of that claim. The balance is hopeless."—*Hostetter's Almanac, 1881.*

"GEORGE, did you ever see the Catskill Mountains?" No, sir, but I have seen them kill mice."—*Ayer's Almanac, 1870.*

A GENTLEMAN took the following telegram to a telegraph office: "Mrs. Brown, Liverpool Street. I announce with grief the death of Uncle James. Come quickly to read his will. I believe we are his heirs. John Black." The clerk, having counted the words, said: "There are two words too many, sir." "All right, cut out 'with grief,' " was the reply.—*Hostetter's Almanac, 1875.*

A FELLOW, who was nearly eaten out of house and home by the constant visit of his friends, was one day complaining bitterly of his numerous visitors. "I can tell you how to get rid of them," said his listener. "Pray, how?" "Lend money to the poor ones, and borrow money from the rich ones, and neither type will ever visit you again."—*Hostetter's Almanac, 1871.*

ONE of the hardest lessons to learn in life is that the man who differs with you, not only in opinions but in principles, may be as honest and sincere as yourself.—*Hostetter's Almanac, 1883.*

TRUST NOT him who seems to be more anxious to give credit than to receive cash.—*Ayer's Almanac, 1869.*

"GEORGE," she said, "before we were married you were always bringing me rings, pins, and things like that. Why don't you bring me anything now?" "My dear," replied George, "did you ever hear of a fisherman feeding bait to a fish he had caught?"—*Hostetter's Almanac, 1892.*

From Rare Coin Review *No. 52, June-September 1984.*

A Treasure for the Future

| By Q. David Bowers | 1970 |

I recently had a telephone call from Jim ——, a sales represen- tative for a large data processing firm. Jim had received our past several catalogues and had placed several orders, including one for a Liberty Seated silver dollar for his type set and another for a Proof Lincoln cent of 1942. "I don't know what I'll do with it, but your price looked appealing, so I am buying it," he said at the time. Another order was for a Bust type half dollar in EF grade.

In each of our telephone calls I detected a vague sense of disorienta- tion with collecting. Jim never seemed to be really sure of what he wanted. During an earlier conversation he mentioned that he wanted to set up an investment fund that would earn 20% as its minimum ob- jective the first year. It seems that he and a few friends had a few extra thousand to "play with," and coins seemed to offer some glamor. Dur- ing that talk I said that I knew of no coins that would be a sure thing so far as earning 20% was concerned. He was disappointed. I could tell by the tone of his voice.

His most recent call was different. "If you have a few moments I would like to tell you something," he started.

"After we last talked I found a numismatic investment counselor, or at least that is what he called himself. He said he would give me a head start on my investment by selling me $1,500 catalogue value worth of coins for $1,000, which would automatically give me a profit of several hundred dollars when I sold them.

"After buying the lot I took it to [a well-known Los Angeles area dealer] and he told me the coins I bought weren't worth full catalogue anyway, and I didn't buy a bargain. In fact he was unkind enough to intimate that the coins weren't worth even $1,000 full retail on an individual basis.

"Following that shock I talked to some others and found out my investment group really was worth about $600 to $700 on a retail basis. What fooled me is that the coins included many selling for under $10 and I didn't realize that a large part of the catalogue value was the dealer's handling cost. I've learned the hard way that if an Uncirculated nickel catalogues 35 cents that doesn't make a roll of them worth 40 times 35 cents or a solid $14.

"I am interested in the reference books you list in your catalogue. It's about time I learned something about coins, I guess." At this point Jim read to me a list of about a half dozen books which he wanted us to set aside for him.

Just as I thought he was ready to say goodbye he said, "May I ask you a favor now that I've just spent about $50 for books?"

"Sure, go ahead," I replied.

"What is going to be 'hot' next in the coin market? I mean, what are all the dealers quietly buying up? I've talked to three other dealers today, and one said he was buying silver futures, another recommended 1970-S Small Date Proof sets, and the other said he didn't know what was going to be the next thing in demand."

I really didn't know how to answer the question. So, my answer was also and "I don't know." I went on to explain that our business made its money by buying coins and reselling them at a markup over the price paid. "We're not investors but, rather, turn our inventory over as quickly as possible. The profits may not be large this way, but they are consistent—and this is what has kept us in business since 1953."

Jim will never be happy with coins. He is looking for something coins do not offer: consistent short-term speculative profits. I wouldn't be surprised if, next year, Jim has forgotten about coins entirely and is investing in some other field which offers a mirage of fast profits without any work or knowledge. Or, maybe I'm wrong. Actually, I hope I am. I hope he reads that $50 worth of books he's bought and takes up coin collecting as a hobby, not primarily as an investment.

The above incident, which happened just a few weeks ago, is not particularly unusual. I have had many similar conversations with other coin "investors." Other dealers, particularly those with over-the-counter trade, have probably heard many more stories than have I. This situation illustrates the frustration of the coin investor who enters coins from a strictly investment viewpoint and cannot grasp that coins are a *collecting* field first and an investment field a distant second.

Mr. Schilke's Experience

Quite different from Jim's experience was the numismatic career of Oscar G. Schilke. Schilke, who passed away several years ago, was a firm friend and advisor for many years.

I first met Oscar at one of the early Metropolitan New York coin conventions in 1954 or 1955. He had read some of my advertisements in *The Numismatic Scrapbook Magazine* and *The Numismatist* and had some coins to offer for sale. If memory serves, they were a few large cents and colonial coins—two or three hundred dollars' worth in all. Oscar never put a price on anything, so I made an offer—which was accepted.

At the time I attended most of the major conventions on the East Coast. At each show Oscar would have five or perhaps a dozen coins for me to see first. He knew that I liked unusual coins, so he would nonchalantly include a surprise in each selection. As I looked through the envelopes he would wait until I came across the special coin and commented on it. On one occasion it was a blazing mint red 1823 large cent, another time it was a large cent with a Washington & Lafayette counterstamp.

In time Mr. and Mrs. Schilke and I became good personal friends in addition to our business acquaintance. Soon, I considered a yearly visit to his tranquil lakeside home in Connecticut to be a "must" on my calendar. During these visits Oscar would tell stories of the "good old days" and the experiences he had with collectors and dealers in the 1930s and 1940s.

Many of Oscar's stories remain in my mind, but one that's particularly vivid concerns his purchases from one of New York City's dealers, Wayte Raymond. This dealer, now deceased, would ask Oscar a certain price for a desired coin and then grant a discount if Oscar could tell him, before buying it, of the coin's background and history!

As did many collectors of the past, Oscar really enjoyed his coins. To aid in appreciating what he purchased and also to learn about coins in general, he built up a large numismatic library. The reference books were purchased, but much of the library just grew over the years as price lists, auction catalogues, periodicals, and so on were added to it. By 1960 the library filled the wall of one room!

During the late 1950s and early 1960s I purchased many of his coins and sets. Oscar would delight in telling me that, "I paid $5 for that one in 1938," as he accepted my offer of $50 for a coin!

Numismatics made Oscar's life richer in many ways. From a pleasure viewpoint he really enjoyed the company of other collectors and dealers, many of whom today can recall his warm hospitality and his love for the coins he owned. From a financial viewpoint, his coin collection made a nice nest egg—an investment whose performance would have been hard to duplicate in any financial medium.

I recall my friendship and business with Oscar to illustrate coins can be rewarding financially, but historically those who have done best have been collectors and numismatists first and investors second.

How Can Success Happen to Me?

"The good old days aren't around anymore, so are the investment opportunities in coins gone also?" This is a logical question which you might ask. In my opinion there are more opportunities than ever. With emphasis on the American citizen having more money in his pocket and more leisure time in which to spend it, the future looms bright for coin collecting and related fields. Coins are a classic example of the supply and demand syndrome. The number of Proof 1911 dimes isn't going to increase (543 of these were made). This particular coin, which I use purely as a random example, catalogues $100 in the 1971 *Guide Book*. By shopping around you can probably find a nice one for about $5 to $10 less. Five years from now if the number of collectors is 50% more than the number today, the price of this coin might well be $120 to $150—or even more if Barber dimes achieve a breakout in popularity, as many series have done over the years. Of course, if the number of collectors decreases, then the price of the dime will decrease, too. This is a factor that always must be considered.

Waiting for the coin market to take its natural course and being there when it happens is one way to make money. A better way to successfully invest is to become a serious numismatist. In this way you not only take advantage of any market rises that might occur, but you can often do well if the market remains stable or advances only slightly.

As an example, for the numismatist who knows what he is looking for there are many "sleepers" just waiting in the pages of the *Guide Book*. If you study coins and the frequency with which they appear on the market, you'll find that many coins listed at low values—including quite a few in the $50 to $300 range—are really extremely rare! You'll also find, I should mention, that certain other coins listed at higher prices are easier to find than some of the cheaper ones!

We don't blame you if you are skeptical at this point. However, let's find some specific examples:

In the 1970 *Guide Book,* the 23rd edition, the 1845-O dime catalogued for just $85 in Uncirculated grade. The catalogue does not invent prices, it reports them. Thus, in many instances in which specific coins have not changed hands for several years or longer, the prices are literally several years or more behind the times. Such was the case of the 1845-O dime. At a coin auction, a wise buyer, despairing of ever finding a mint condition dime of this variety and knowing how rare the coin was in that grade, bought one for over $800! Yes, that's about 10 times catalogue. Really, this was not surprising or even unexpected to anyone who had studied the Liberty Seated dime series—as evidently at least two people (the purchaser and the underbidder) in that sale had done. Now the 24th edition of the catalogue simply has a dash in the Uncirculated column for the 1845-O. Had you been aware of the rarity of the Uncirculated 1845-O last year, perhaps you could have found one somewhere for around catalogue value. Now the cat is out of the bag and that possibility is gone.

Walter Breen, the numismatic researcher, has made thousands of dollars by finding bargains—especially with die varieties purchased from dealers who didn't attribute them or didn't know what they had.

We recently paid $3,000 for a coin which, two years ago, was purchased for $15 from a dealer! It was a rare colonial die variety. Similarly, dealer James Ruddy recently told me of an instance in which a rare variety worth some $600 to $700 was found by a scout for $10 at a coin show!

For illustrative purposes, here are some coins for which we'll gladly pay over the catalogue value: 1785 Immune Columbia Vermont cent, all grades; 1786 Baby Head Vermont, Fine; 1787 Nova Eborac (New York) coinage, all varieties, Very Fine; 1828 12 Stars half cent, Uncirculated; 1817 cent, 15 Star variety, Uncirculated; any Uncirculated "O" mint half dime of the 1840s; any Proof Liberty Seated silver dollar in the 1840s, and a Proof $20 of 1858. We could add dozens more coins to the list. We're not offering to pay over catalogue to be philanthropic: we know we can make a profit over and above what we pay.

Form a Collection

The best way to learn about coins and to have fun at the same time is to form a collection. If you want to sample the flavor of all United States coins, try a type set. Or, you may want to specialize.

As an example of a specialized collection, let's assume that you want to collect a set of Uncirculated and Proof Liberty Seated half dimes from 1837 to 1873. We'll also assume that you're willing to pay full catalogue if necessary, but hope to buy quite a few for less.

By writing to a half dozen or a dozen leading dealers you should be able to get all or nearly all of the Proofs from 1859 to 1873. Chances are you'll buy none of the earlier 1855-1858 ones. These will require some patience. Among the expensive Uncirculated issues you'll probably buy an 1837 No Stars issue. You'll probably have the chance to buy several of these. You'll rightly guess that the $275 catalogue price is due to other factors. In this instance, although there are a fair number of Uncirculated 1837 half dimes around, there is a tremendous demand for them, not by half dime collectors, but by type set collectors. You'll find no Uncirculated 1838-O half dimes offered.

You'll buy some of the Philadelphia Mint Uncirculated coins of the 1840s and a few of the San Francisco issues of the 1860s and 1870s. You'll buy the expensive ($900) 1860 transitional issue as there are always a few on the market. You'll not hear even a whisper of the availability of the 1842-O, 1844-O, 1846, 1853-O Without Arrows, or the 1859 transitional in Mint State. Even though you might tell a dealer, "I'll pay full catalogue," the answer will be: "I haven't had any of those in a long time."

After working on your specialized half dime collection for a year you'll still have quite a few empty spaces. You'll have had a lot of fun collecting the pieces you did find and you'll really appreciate those you lack as you get them in the future one by one.

When completed, if you are successful in getting all of the pieces, you will have a first-class numismatic investment. There's not a dealer in the country who wouldn't be eager to buy it! As the rarity of certain of the earlier issues becomes known (remember the 1845-O dime situation we mentioned a few paragraphs ago) you'll find, over the years, that some pieces you have, say $100 invested in, can be sold for $400 or $500. The chances are excellent that you'll make a nice profit overall.

From Rare Coin Review *No. 7, September 1970.*

Collect With a Purpose

By Q. David Bowers   1984

W hat to collect? Undoubtedly this question has run through your mind if you are a typical numismatist. The vast panorama of American coinage offers many possibilities. Liberty Walking half dollars are attractive, Barber dimes form a challenge, Morgan dollars are high on the popularity list, Vermont copper coins of 1785-1788 seem interesting, and there are hundreds of other possibilities.

Why collect with a purpose? Why not just accumulate coins? In the writer's opinion, to do so would be to lose much of the fun numismatics has to offer. Around 20 years ago a gentleman named Terrell commissioned my firm to build for him a type set of United States copper, nickel, and silver coins. Not being inclined to be a collector, he considered investment to be his prime objective. Still, he wanted something that was oriented with a plan in mind, something with a purpose. We suggested a type set would be ideal, and he followed our advice. Looking over our shoulder, so to speak, he watched us buy for him superb early American silver coins, Uncirculated and Proof Liberty Seated and Barber coins, and numerous other pieces which comprise such a grouping. After much effort on our part, and after a good deal of check-writing on his, the type set approached completion. No, it did not have one of each and every design type in the finest possible condition, but it came fairly close. His interest turned in other directions, and he commissioned us to sell his holdings. An auction catalogue bearing the inscription *Terrell Collection* was issued. Perhaps you remember it. The offering of such a fantastic grouping of United States coins attracted considerable attention, and when the hammer had fallen on the last lot,

"The price record book had to be thrown out the window," as one observer said. Many new realizations were set. In the process our consignor reaped a rich return on his original expenditure. A businessman with his fingers in many pies, the consignor told me that no investment in his lifetime had yielded such a high return. Just before I wrote this article I telephoned him to say "hello," and he mentioned that since his collection was sold (something he regrets, as it would be worth much more now!) he has not had another investment which equaled it.

The Terrell Collection was an instance of two plus two equaling more than four. The coins in the group, while desirable on an individual basis, were worth more as a *collection*. True, the collection was not sold intact; it was broken up. But, the collection was offered all at once, and this is what attracted so many people. Similarly, when the Garrett Collection was auctioned by my firm in 1979 through 1981 the prices realized were substantially over the market value, mainly because bidders wanted to own an item with the Garrett pedigree.

As you chart your numismatic course, I recommend that you have some sort of a plan. Type set collecting is a popular way to go. A modest budget can be stretched a long way in this fashion. When your coins are sold—and everyone sells someday—you will find that a *collection* of coins is worth more than an *accumulation*. At least that's my opinion.

Specialization is another route. There are many challenges within the field of United States coins. Some pieces which seem to be common really aren't once you look for them. In the current issue of the *Rare Coin Review* (No. 50, January-March 1984) we list a wide array of Barber half dollars for sale from the 1892-1915 years. These are not MS-65 or Proof-65 pieces but, for the most part, are graded Extremely Fine and AU. And yet we make the claim in that listing that the pieces are elusive, hard to find, seldom seen. This may sound strange coming from the pen of a cataloguer who has described 1804 silver dollars, 1827 original quarters, 1787 Brasher doubloons, and the like. While EF and AU Barber half dollars aren't in the category of those landmark rarities, still within the context of coinage of the past century they are more difficult to track down than the somewhat nominal catalogue values indicate. Try putting together a set of EF to AU Barber halves. There are no "impossible" rarities, but there are some strong challenges! Liberty nickels offer a somewhat similar challenge. No, I can't say that we have a detailed listing of EF and AU Liberty nickels in this catalogue, for we don't, but this doesn't mean that you shouldn't make a beginning here, perhaps filling out your set with some future offerings.

Sometimes specialized sets can be made within a given area. Thus when a Washington numismatist telephoned to express an interest in Liberty Walking half dollars, I suggested that rather than buy three or four each of a half dozen different dates, he commence building a collection from 1934 through 1947, a "collection." In this way, I reasoned, he could form a display that would be meaningful and interesting. Tom Becker told me of a West Coast client, actually a *prospective* client (when he first called), who contacted him with the idea of spending around $25,000 on commemorative coins. His initial inclination was to buy five to 10 pieces each of four or five different dates, but Tom steered him in the direction of building a type set. By the time you read these words, our West Coast *friend* (for we have come to know him quite well through our telephone conversations) will have one of the nicest type sets in existence of commemorative half dollars from 1892 onward. And, at this point he lacks just a few pieces. This is far more interesting, to my way of thinking, than having a dozen or so 1935 Hudson half dollars (or some other scarcity) and no others!

Perhaps the Carson City Mint interests you. A number of collectors have opted to acquire Morgan dollars of the Carson City years from 1878 through 1885 and again from 1889 through 1893. Indeed, plastic holders are available shaped like Nevada and with appropriate spaces for each of these issues. With the connotation of the Comstock Lode, such Carson City silver dollars have an interesting romantic flavor to them. Curiously, I don't recall anyone aspiring to collect Morgan dollars from New Orleans only but there is no reason why such a grouping cannot be put together. Silver dollars from Philadelphia only or San Francisco only present additional opportunities.

Among commemorative half dollars it is possible to build a type set or a date and variety set. These methods are well known. However, within this series one can build mini-type sets. For example, with my copy of *A Guide Book of United States Coins* in my hand I note that a collection of Civil War related commemoratives could be formed to include the following: 1937 Antietam, 1918 Illinois (with Abraham Lincoln's portrait on the obverse), 1925 Stone Mountain, and in a related way, representative Booker T. Washington and Washington-Carver issues. Topical collecting, or collecting by design motifs, is very popular among stamp collectors, but for some reason it has never caught on with numismatists. Still, there are some possibilities. In the field of commemorative half dollars further consider, for example, that the following issues depict different types of ships: 1936 Bay Bridge, 1892-1893 Columbian, 1936 Delaware, 1935 Hudson, 1924 Huguenot, 1936 Long Island, 1936 Norfolk, 1920-1921 Pilgrim, and 1936 Rhode Island. Commemorative half dollars pertaining to New England, issues pertaining to exploration in the West, and other categories represent still further possibilities. As still another example I mention that I have never seen a collection of commemorative half dollars limited only to issues produced at the Denver Mint.

When you plan your collecting objectives, a sense of *market strategy* is helpful. It is oft times desirable to collect what no one else seems interested in. This takes some willpower to do, for it is ever so easy to follow the crowd. Collect something that is being promoted or trumpeted, and you feel you are in good company and you are "doing the right thing." However, at the same time you are probably paying a strong market price. March to the beat of a different drummer, and prices are apt to be less expensive, competition will be less intense, and you have a better chance of completion. In numismatics every series has its turn whether it be commemoratives, silver dollars, Barber issues, Liberty Seated coins, Capped Bust half dollars of 1807-1836, tokens of George Washington, or whatever. Collect now, and when the time comes to sell, the market in your particular area of interest may well be much stronger, to your obvious financial reward.

Right now colonial and state coins are quiet in the marketplace. Why is this? First, in general these pieces have suffered from a lack of publicity. Scarcely a single investment newsletter or market "expert" recommends them! Indeed, most numismatic writers in this vein would not know a *Double Head* Washington token from a plugged Hibernia farthing! Second, right now the field is missing some of the great individuals who have helped build the market. John Roper, one of the country's leading colonial specialists, and Richard Picker, the foremost specialist dealer in the area, both passed away about a year ago. Ted Craige, another super-collector, also is no longer with us. The voids left by these gentlemen have yet to be filled. Current market popularity trends point toward MS-65 and Proof-65 conditions, something entirely possible in the field of Liberty Walking half dollars, Morgan dollars, and other issues of the past century, but grades seldom seen among colonial and early United States issues. "If it is not MS-65, I won't buy it!" I have seen beginning collectors take this stance more than once. Denied to such collectors, then, is the entire field of copper coinage of Vermont, Massachusetts, Connecticut, New York, and New Jersey of the 1785-1788 era, unquestionably one of the most numismatically fascinating of all collecting areas.

Another interesting way to collect would be to assemble a group of coins with interesting stories. Such a grouping would be somewhat like a type set, but it would not necessarily have one of each design type represented. What is an interesting story to me might not be an interesting story to you, so such a collection would have an intensely personal characteristic. I like the 1909 V.D.B. Lincoln cent, an inexpensive piece but one which certainly played an important part in American numismatic history. On the other end of the price scale is the MCMVII (1907) High Relief double eagle, an expensive and beautiful coin representing the work that noted sculptor Augustus Saint-Gaudens did at the request of President Theodore Roosevelt. In between are many other interesting pieces such as the 1883 Without CENTS nickel, the 1938-D/S Overmintmark nickel (the first such overmintmark to be discovered), and so on. Three of our friends and clients have specialized in the coins of a single year, 1873. Harry X Boosel started things going a long time ago when he wrote a series of articles on 1873 coins for the *Numismatic Scrapbook Magazine*. Roy Harte, one of our favorite numismatists (he has consigned three separate collections to us for sale at auction!), formed a beautiful collection of the 1873 year, as did a commercial firm, Royal Coins. Have you ever thought about collecting the coins of your birth year? If you were born before 1940, such a collection might be more difficult and extensive than you might at first think! Consider, for example, that a set of 1938 coins contains not only Philadelphia, Denver, and San Francisco examples of the cent, nickel, dime, quarter, and half dollar, but also includes a number of commemoratives. On the other hand, a set of 1949, 1953, or later coins would be easier to put together.

If you have no coins at all, then I recommend that you acquire coins of different design types. For example, rather than buying a half dozen different Barber half dollars, buy one Barber half dollar, one Barber dime, one Barber quarter, and so on—as these will fit nicely into a type set of United States coin designs. Later, if you want to specialize then you can build a set by date and mintmark varieties. If you have decided upon a specialization, say Morgan silver dollars, then buy as many different issues as possible, *do not* buy just a group of five or 10 of a single date or mintmark variety to the exclusion of others.

Form a meaningful collection—whether it be a type set, a date set, or whatever—and when time comes to sell you will be far ahead of your fellow numismatists. As an auctioneer of important coin properties over a long period of years, time and time again I have seen great excitement shown when *collections* are offered for sale.

From Rare Coin Review *No. 50, January-March 1984.*

Interesting Aspects of Coin Grading

By James F. Ruddy   1974

Coin Grading and Its Importance

The condition or grading of a coin is extremely important. The oft asked question "What is it worth?" is dependent to a large degree upon how much wear a particular coin has received. When it leaves the coining press a coin is in "new" condition—a grade which collectors designate as "Uncirculated," or a coin which has never seen circulation. Such a coin is brilliant and frosty and shows no sign of wear or use. After a coin has been used in the channels of commerce for many years—possibly for 50 years or more—it becomes extremely worn. Often coins are encountered which are almost illegible due to the amount of wear they have received. These coins would be at the opposite end of the scale—and would grade what collectors call "About Good." In between these extremes there are many other conditions. In order from the lowest to the highest the standard conditions are: About Good, Good, Very Good, Fine, Very Fine, Extremely Fine, About Uncirculated, and Uncirculated. And then there is a special condition—a condition which describes a coin with a mirrorlike surface struck especially for collectors—Proof.

I might mention at this point that it is common practice to capitalize the grade of a coin. Thus a coin description such as, "I offer you an

1835 half dollar in Fine condition" means not that the coin is "fine" in the sense of being "nice" or "desirable" but, rather, is "Fine" as per strict grading standards defining that term. This capitalization serves to prevent confusion.

As a collector or investor, grading will be extremely important to you. Next to the information on the coin (such as the date, mintmark, or denomination) the grade is the single most important factor you must know in order to determine a coin's true market value. Any catalogue or pricing guide will give you a range of current values, but for any given coin these values will depend upon the condition. As one of many illustrations I could cite, I mention the case of a 1920 half dollar. In 1973 the *Guide Book of United States Coins* valued a 1920 half dollar at $1.25 in Good condition. In Very Good condition the same coin was worth $1.75. Fine, the piece brought $45; Very Fine $7; and Extremely Fine $13.50. An Uncirculated or like-new 1920 half dollar brought $110. There is a tremendous difference between the $1.25 price for a Good piece and the $110 price for an Uncirculated coin—one piece is dozens of times more valuable than the other! Other coins have even more dramatic price differentials. An extremely worn 1794 large cent is worth about $40 in Good condition. In Uncirculated condition the same piece would be worth several thousand dollars!

The importance of correctly grading coins cannot be stressed too much. As a coin buyer you should no sooner accept a coin in Fine condition while paying a Very Fine price than you would accept a coin with a different date or mintmark than the one you specifically ordered. The value of each individual coin is largely determined by its grade. As noted earlier, it is not uncommon to find a difference of many dollars, or even many hundreds of dollars in value from one grade to another. Coin grading is thus too important to be dependent on instinct or guesswork. A standard system is necessary.

The basic rules should be such that every dealer and collector can abide by them. A coin is designated by a specific grade in accordance with the amount of wear it has received. This condition should not change because of transfer from one owner to another. Unfortunately, when buying a coin some might grade a particular specimen as being in Fine condition—but after owning it and then deciding to sell it, it magically (or, perhaps "hopefully" would be a better word) becomes Very Fine! Such practices can be eliminated by wide-spread knowledge of grading.

In the field of numismatic research, grading is likewise useful. Common grading terminology permits the interchange of information in a concise manner. A scholar doing research on rare 1793 one-cent pieces will know that he has made an extremely important discovery if he locates a particular variety in Extremely Fine condition, if the next best specimen of this variety grades only Very Good. By using common grading terminology our researcher knows he has made an important find without even seeing the next best coin—for Extremely Fine fits certain standards and Very Good fits other standards—thus permitting an interchange of information.

Coin grading, extremely important today, has not always been so. People have been collecting coins for over 2,000 years—making numismatics one of the oldest hobbies in the world. Before the 20th century most collectors classified either coins as being either new or used. Rarely did the price of a coin dictate that a finer distinction in grading be made. Most United States coins, including some great scarcities and rarities, could be purchased for a small premium over their face value.

The story today is much different. In recent decades there has been an ever-increasing demand for rare coins. The supply of rare coins remains constant since the mintage of a given year can never be changed. The natural result has been a dramatic appreciation in value. It thus became increasingly more important to grade coins carefully. Where a difference between Good and Fine grade might have meant $25 to $50 in the 1960s, it meant at least $50 to $100 by the mid-1970s.

In earlier years it was possible to grade a coin by "instinct" or by experience. No grading guides were available, or, for that matter, were even necessary—for (as I have noted earlier) coins were not collected by condition. Likewise, coins were not collected by minor varieties or even by mintmark varieties until the 20th century. It may come as a surprise to learn that during the 19th century, collectors cared little whether a coin bore an "S," "C," or other mintmark!

Today the market is much more sophisticated. In recent decades many important and valuable guides have appeared on the market. While the list of such books is a long one, there are a number of publications that are important for the important impact they have on the collecting field. The *Standard Catalogue*, first released in the early 1930s, made possible the dissemination periodically (catalogues were issued every year or so) of pricing knowledge. Prior to this time reference books containing pricing information were not generally available—and to determine a coin's value a collector had to discuss

values with other collectors, read price lists and auction records, and
so on. The *Standard Catalogue* provided instant information in a convenient volume. In 1947 *A Guide Book of United States Coins,* written
by R.S. Yeoman and published by Whitman Publishing Company, first
appeared. Since that time this book, issued yearly, has achieved total
sales of over 10 million copies—making it one of the most successful
nonfiction books ever published! Numismatic periodicals spearheaded
by *The Numismatist* (first published in 1888 and adopted as the official
publication of the American Numismatic Association in 1892) was joined
in 1935 by *The Numismatic Scrapbook* magazine, a monthly publication. In 1952 *Numismatic News,* first bi-weekly (and in more recent
years weekly) made its debut. In 1960 came *Coin World,* a weekly publication which soon grew to enjoy an audience of over 100,000 readers.
The "Tele-Quotes" section of *Numismatic News,* and the "Trends of
United States Coins" part of *Coin World* have made available pricing
information on a weekly basis in recent years. Other magazines,
notably *CoinAge* and *Coins Magazine,* have provided additional information.

However, in the field of coin grading, much less progress has been
made. In 1958 Messrs. Brown and Dunn pioneered the standardization
of grading by issuing a book which used line drawings to illustrate degrees of wear on a coin. A number of attempts to create standard
reference works by using photographs of actual coins were made by
others. Unfortunately, the photographic reproduction, and in a few
cases, the grading information, was inadequate to warrant the acceptance of any of these works as a standard.

Therefore, in the 1960s, collectors were faced with the paradox of
having excellent progress in pricing information but very little that was
new in grading guidelines since 1958. As noted, grading is extremely
important, as the value of a coin depends not only on its date and mintmark but on its condition. All of these fine pricing guides were not
much use if constant quarrels resulted when a buyer and seller had a
different opinion as to the grade of a coin. My own experience in coins
began in 1953. By the mid-1960s my business had grown to the point
at which I had handled virtually every rarity listed in the *Guide Book
of United States Coins,* had sold millions of dollars' worth of specimens
to collectors all over the world, and had handled some of the most important collections to have come on the market. Still, the problem of
grading bothered me. I felt that I knew grading quite well and, indeed,
I never had much of a problem with the subject. However, correspondence with others indicated that grading was a sticky point in

many coin transactions. So, I decided to devote several years to writing a book that would fill the need for standardized photographic grading information.

I knew that a number of factors were necessary to produce a successful photographic grading guide. First was access to the hundreds of thousands of dollars worth of coins needed for photography. When all was said and done several years later I actually ended up taking pictures of coins worth over $300,000—and close to half of these were pictured in the *Photograde* book. For two years I systematically took pictures of every coin that came through my hands which represented the average of its grade for its type. Realizing that it might take forever and a day to get each and every coin type in each and every condition if I relied upon pieces coming through my own stock, I enlisted the help of others. While literally dozens of people assisted me in various regards, I might mention that Jerry Cohen, Abner Kreisberg, Jan Bronson, Joe Flynn, Jr., and my long-time business associate, Q. David Bowers, helped me the most.

It was enjoyable, of course, to photograph expensive rarities. However, some of the most interesting situations arose when grading cheap coins. I went from coin show to coin show and from dealer to dealer with a "want list" of coins I needed to complete the book. It was sometimes embarrassing to search through a dealer's "junk box" for an About Good Jefferson nickel or Lincoln cent that might have a retail value of scarcely more than its face value! Knowing that I handled many of America's greatest rarities and enjoyed one of the most successful coin businesses in the United States, most dealers were positive that I had "something up my sleeve" when I spent an hour looking through coins that were virtually worthless! In fact, most dealers thought I had some new and very valuable discovery that I was keeping secret from them—and many were reluctant to sell me a low-grade coin from their "junk box" thinking that it might be a great rarity in disguise! In one case a dealer actually spent five minutes scrutinizing a coin for which he had an asking price of 15 cents before selling it to me. It happened to be a 1905 Barber dime in About Good grade! "Why is a dealer who has handled 1913 Liberty nickels, 1894-S dimes, 1876-CC 20-cent pieces (all of which are worth tens of thousands of dollars today) spending his valuable time looking at a 15-cent dime?" was undoubtedly running through his mind. I might mention that I did not publicize the *Photograde* project while working on it—for having to explain my research would have only compounded the problem as I visited dozens of dealers.

Another important factor in formulating the *Photograde* system was adhering to strict research standards. Fortunately I had many years of professional coin dealing experience to draw from. In this time I graded many millions of dollars' worth of coins—probably far more than any normal scholar could have ever hoped to have examined at close range. In addition, I was helped by my schooling and professional training which originally was in the field of scientific research. This background taught me to be precise and methodical and to consider very minute details—factors which are vitally important when formulating a universal grading system.

One of the most formidable factors to conquer was that of photography. The main problem was the extremes involved—the wide range of detail from About Good to About Uncirculated; the size differential from tiny silver three-cent pieces to huge silver dollars; and the variations in toning from a dark, porous copper surface to a brilliant, shiny silver or gold surface. Again, I was fortunate to have a background which was of immeasurable help. Before coins became my career I worked in the Physics Research Laboratory of the Ansco Film Company where I performed research on all types of photographic film. Even with this extensive experience it took many weeks of research to match the right camera, film, and light metering devices to produce the desired results. The film I finally picked was an extremely high resolution, high contrast, very fine grain film. The desire was not to take a "pretty picture" but to take an informative picture. I wanted film that would show every hairline detail so that people using the *Photograde* book would have nothing left to the imagination. Controversy, long something that went hand-in-hand with coin grading, was to be eliminated, in my opinion. In retrospect I can now say that *Photograde* has been extremely successful in this regard—and has helped resolve the controversy that once existed.

Lighting the coin was of paramount importance when photographing it. Hundreds of test exposures utilizing dozens of various lighting conditions were tried before the first coin picture was taken. Experiments in film processing, background color, and the size of the printed coin picture were also necessary. Believe it or not, I took over 5,000 photographs to achieve the end results! This task was immense. Each coin had to be positioned and lighted separately with a fine degree of accuracy. Often it was very difficult to correctly light the area of the coin that was to be described to define that grade; to light that particular portion without casting shadows on the rest of the coin. So many times I would choose a coin which seemed to perfectly represent the average grade I was looking for only to find, when the final print was obtained, that the camera didn't see it my way—and I would have to start all over again! For one particular coin grade and variety I had to use 22 different coins before coming up with one that photographed perfectly! The final word on the finished *Photograde* was from an executive of Whitman Publishing Company, publishers of the highly successful *Guide Book of United States Coins.* "We wanted to issue a photographic grading guide, but simply knew of no way of taking all of the pictures that would be necessary," I was told.

Another important factor was the printing. Much time was spent arranging the pictures and working with the printer to insure that the photographs would be produced with the finest processes commercially available. An extremely fine line screen was needed in order to show up the sharp details that were evident in my original photographs. Naturally this resulted in quite a bit of extra expense—but it is gratifying that the results have been worth it, and the resultant *Photograde* book displays the illustrations almost as sharply as it would if I included my original photographs directly!

What happened to *Photograde* after it was released? To say that it was enthusiastically received would be an understatement. My first printing was quickly sold out, as was my second printing, my third, my fourth, and so on! While the sales were certainly most impressive and most gratifying (and continue to be to this very day as more and more collectors learn about the worth of the *Photograde* book), some of the most pleasurable moments were afforded by the comments of my associates and acquaintances in numismatics. Every major numismatic publication had nice things to say about the book! The advertising department of *Coin World,* the largest publication in the coin hobby field, even sent me a congratulatory telegram—and ordered six copies for the use of its staff! Was *Photograde* profitable to me? This depends on how you look at the situation. From a financial viewpoint it is entirely possible that the same thousands of hours, if spent buying and selling coins as part of my regular business, could have produced more in terms of actual profit. However, no amount of coin sales could have produced as much satisfaction. Here is a factor that transcends financial considerations.

How To Grade Your Coins

Actual grading information on a coin-by-coin basis is found in my

Photograde book—which I modestly recommend as an interesting, as well as a financially important, addition to your numismatic lilbrary—just as *A Guide Book of United States Coins* will be a basic tool when you price coins. However, it certainly would be appropriate to give some basic grading considerations here.

The basic lowest condition used by collectors is the About Good classification. This represents a very well-worn coin which can still be identified as to date and mint. The date will be visible in its entirety, or at least the significant digits (such as the last one or two numerals) will be present in order to identify it without equivocation. The mint-mark, even though it might be worn so as to only be a blob or an indication, will still be identifiable. I might mention at this point that lower grades are sometimes used—descriptions such as Fair and Poor are occasionally used to describe coins which only have a tiny portion of the designs visible. For instance, you might be able to tell that a given coin in Poor condition is indeed a United States Indian cent—but you might not have the foggiest notion of what date it is! So, About Good represents the minimum that a collector will usually accept for his collection—for the coin can then be identified as to the place and time in which it was minted.

Next up the grading ladder is Good grade. This usually indicates an over-all clean-appearing coin which has all or nearly all lettering visible and basic features outlined, except for certain coins dated in the 1700s and early 1800s.

Very Good is a popular intermediate grade. It is also one of the easiest grades to classify. Although the description of Very Good varies from one coin design to another, in the majority of cases the word "LIBERTY" on the headband or on the shield can be used to determine this grade. On many different coin designs it is stated that a total of any three letters of the word "LIBERTY" serve to identify a coin as being in Very Good grade. The total of three letters can consist of three separate letters, or perhaps two full letters and two half letters, or even one full letter and an equivalent number of partial letters. Of course, it is important that all other features of both the obverse and reverse verify this grade as well. If just the distinctive letters of the word "LIBERTY" were to show but if the date or mintmark were not visible then the coin would, of course, grade less!

Fine condition is probably the most widely collected circulated condition. All of the major design is usually visible. The word "LIBERTY" (except on 20-cent pieces and on certain silver dollar varieties) is complete. Fine condition often represents an attractive compromise between the cost of a coin and the availability of all the design features. Thus it is a very popular condition—and many collect by this grade.

Up the grading scale one more notch is Very Fine. More of the intricate designs will be noticeable than on a coin in Fine condition. We are now getting into a technical realm—and it is difficult to give here the distinguishing differences. The comparison of actual coins or coin photographs serves to define the grade.

Next comes Extremely Fine or, as people sometimes say, "Extra Fine" (although "extra" is not really an appropriate term, for "extra" means "superfluous"). Nearly all of the design details will be visible on an Extremely Fine coin. This is a coin that has seen limited circulation—possibly for just a few years.

Next comes About Uncirculated. This is a coin which is nearly Uncirculated—a piece which has only been circulated for a short period of time. Often some mint lustre will show in the field and in protected spaces of the coin such as areas between letters.

Uncirculated coins are those which have not seen actual circulation in hand-to-hand use in commerce. To be sure, collectors recognize several variations of the Uncirculated grade. The term Brilliant Uncirculated describes a piece which has full mint color. A coin which acquired toning over the years is described as being Toned Uncirculated, Red and Brown Uncirculated, or any other adjectives which describe its coloration. Toning on some coins is quite beautiful—and occasionally picturesque descriptions such as "a lovely lilac toned Proof 1876 quarter with iridescent hues" will be used to describe such a piece in a sale catalogue.

Certain early coins are extremely difficult to find in Uncirculated condition without any bagmarks or handling marks. Such flawless pieces are sometimes designated as Choice Uncirculated or Gem Uncirculated. Choice describes an above average Uncirculated specimen, well struck and with a minimum of minor bagmarks or minting defects. Gem Uncirculated is the finest available—a sharply struck coin which is free of the usual minor bagmarks or minting defects.

Another description often used is Brilliant Uncirculated with light rubbing. This is a coin with full mint lustre which may show some rubbing, particularly on the very highest parts, due to rubbing from an album slide in a coin collection, or by rubbing against other coins in a mint bag.

It must be remembered that coins are produced for commercial purposes—to provide a medium of exchange in commerce and trade.

Mints of the past and present, faced with working long hours to satisfy an ever-increasing demand for such pieces, cannot afford to mint coins carefully so far as collectors are concerned. Let us consider, for instance, a typical coin—a $20 gold piece minted at Carson City, Nevada in 1883. The coin, when first minted, was ejected from the coining press and dropped into a hopper of other $20 gold pieces. Immediately the surface acquired several nicks and other marks from contact with other pieces. Our new coin was then dumped from the hopper, possibly inspected for any minting defects (such as a faulty planchet), and then put with other coins mixed loosely in a bag. During these production processes no care was taken to handle the coin by its edges or otherwise give it the care that a collector would have. To have done so would have tremendously increased the mintage expense! Once bagged, the coin would have been transferred, possibly a long distance, to a storage area in a bank. It then might have moved from bank to bank several times during the next few decades. For purposes of our illustration here, we will assume that the coin never was released into official channels of commerce but was, say, obtained from a bank for use as a Christmas gift many years ago. Even though our 1883-CC double eagle is technically Uncirculated, it is evident from the handling that it has received that it will show some handling marks. In fact, as you might suspect from the preceding description, to find an 1883-CC double eagle (or any other early double eagle from this far-West mint) in Gem Uncirculated condition would be virtually impossible.

On the other hand, a small coin such as a modern dime is of much lighter weight and can more easily survive the rigors of bank-to-bank or intra-mint handling. So, finding a modern coin in Gem Uncirculated condition is not usually difficult.

Proof represents another coin grade. Proof is not a "superior" grade to "Uncirculated" but, rather, is a different grade. Proof coins are those struck especially for collectors. Special dies, dies polished to a high mirrorlike finish, are used. Special planchets (blank metal pieces) are likewise carefully treated before the designs are impressed on them. The result is a specially-created coin with a mirrorlike or a Proof surface. When a Proof coin becomes worn (as it might be if someone inadvertently "spends" it!) it does not then become "Uncirculated" or "Almost Uncirculated," as the coin never was Uncirculated in the first place. This distinction is often overlooked by collectors. Rather, a Proof which has seen wear is best described as being an "impaired Proof." Of course, if the wear is such that all of the Proof surface is gone then it can be graded by normal lower grades such as Fine, Very Fine, and so on.

Proofs were made in a number of styles. During the early 20th century the Philadelphia Mint experimented with several different types of Proof finishes: including Satin Proof, Sandblast Proof, and Matte Proof. Although the manufacturing processes differ from one another, these terms are sometimes used interchangeably today. These types of Proofs have a grainy surface that serves to highlight the higher parts of the coins in almost a medallic relief. Recognizing a Matte Proof and being able to distinguish it from an Uncirculated coin is important. Sometimes there does not appear to be a great difference to the untrained eye. However, Matte Proofs invariably have sharp, squared-off rims which serve to differentiate them.

The standard type of Proof is that with the "brilliant" surface. These are the Proofs minted with the mirrorlike dies as described earlier. Although specimens with prooflike characteristics occur from earlier years, equipment for the production of Brilliant Proof coins was first installed in the Philadelphia Mint in 1817 (during which year certain equipment was installed to replace that lost or damaged in the Mint fire of 1816). From 1817 through the early 1850s, Proofs were produced only on infrequent occasions—mainly for presentation to government officials, dignitaries, and so on. Collectors could obtain them upon special request—but there were not very many collectors at that time, so the numbers minted were small. It might be appropriate to note here that in the year 1827, pioneer collector J.J. Mickley went to the Philadelphia Mint and obtained four 1827 Proof quarters for the face value of 25c each. Today each of these coins would bring more than $20,000 on the collectors' market! Proof coins were first regularly offered for sale in 1858. In that year only 80 sets were sold. Contrast that figure to the 3 to 4 million sets produced on the average during the late 1960s and early 1970s!

For purposes of conciseness, abbreviations are often used to designate coin grades. About Good is often abbreviated as "Abt. G" or "AG." Good is abbreviated simply as "G" and Very Good as "VG." Fine is abbreviated as "F"; Very Fine as "VF"; and Extremely Fine as "EF" (or sometimes as "XF"). About Uncirculated is conveniently shortened to "AU." Uncirculated often is seen as "Unc." Brilliant Uncirculated is commonly abbreviated as "BU." Proof is shortened to "Pr." occasionally.

Some Comments Concerning Grading

Strange as it may seem, one coin can often be correctly described as being in two different grades! The obverse or front side of a coin might be in Extremely Fine condition (as an example) while the reverse is in just Fine condition! How is this so? The answer is simple: Many coins, particularly ones from the 18th and 19th centuries, were struck with different degrees of die detail and relief. Take for instance a certain variety of 1794 cent. The obverse or front side of the coin was struck with a high relief, almost like a sculpture or a medal. Less attention was given to the reverse side of the coin—and all of the designs were cut very shallowly. The rim around the coin, while present, was very low. After the coin had been in circulation for 20 or 30 years the reverse was worn considerably as the features weren't very distinct to begin with. On the other hand, the obverse features, being protected from wear by the high rim, wore to a much lesser extent. The result was that the coin today might be accurately described as having an Extremely Fine obverse and a Fine reverse. Many other examples occur. This particular coin could be described in abbreviated form as being in EF/F condition. The obverse grading, always listed first, is EF. The diagonal mark then separates the obverse grade from the reverse grade, which is Fine.

When you take into consideration that early coins were made from hand-crafted dies it is apparent that some features used in grading will vary from issue to issue. On certain varieties of 1795 half cents the date was cut into the die so lightly that even specimens in AU grade have the date scarcely visible! On the other hand, 1807 one-cent pieces had the date cut into the dies so heavily that specimens in About Good condition have the date showing extremely boldly.

Colonial coins are even a better case in point. Gake as an example the colonial coins of Connecticut. From 1785 through 1788 the state of Connecticut produced its own copper coinage. This was not done by an official state mint, but, rather, was assigned to private contractors. The coins of the first year, 1785, were struck carefully for the most part and show the details in sharp relief. The planchets are fairly round and the dies were carefully cut. The planchets were heavy and contained a goodly amount of metal. It was soon realized that more profit could be obtained if the dies were made more hurriedly and if less attention was paid to the correct metal content. So, the inevitable happened: the dies were made more and more quickly and with less and less detail as the years went by. The planchets were carelessly prepared and often were not even completely round! Specimens of the last year of Connecticut coinage, 1788, often were very weakly struck and sometimes had large parts of the designs or lettering missing when first issued! It is such variations that make collecting of Connecticut coins (and other colonial issues) interesting to the numismatist. To many, such pieces have a fantastic degree of "romance" attached to them. However, from a grading standpoint it is very important to note that one cannot grade a Connecticut cent of 1785 by the same standards as one of 1788. Other examples abound in numismatics.

When grading any coin it is important to consider the coin "on the average." As noted in the preceding paragraph, variations in the particular die variety or the striking of that variety must be taken into consideration—especially with earlier issues. The reader must average out the plus and minus factors when grading a coin. If an early one-cent piece, for example, shows weak letters on the left side of the coin and very strong letters on the right side of the coin, it must be assumed that the coin could not have been worn only on one portion of its surface over the years! Rather, the entire coin must be averaged in order to arrive at a grade. When you grade a particular coin take into consideration all of the features on each side—and not just an isolated weak spot which may have been the result of striking and not of wear.

Proper Cleaning and Care for Your Coins

The subject of cleaning interests many collectors and dealers. At the outset I might mention that more coins have been damaged by cleaning than have been improved by cleaning—so be careful! Cleaning any coin that grades less than About Uncirculated will generally produce an unnatural appearance that is not acceptable to most collectors. The cleaning of copper coins in any grade should be avoided unless it is absolutely necessary in order to remove an unsightly fingerprint or large carbon or corrosion spots.

When cleaning coins use only a clear liquid "dip," not a paste, powder, or polish. It is important to think independently in this regard—for many manufacturers of paste and polish advertise heavily in order to sell their products—without regard to the tremendous amount of damage that many such products can inflict upon coins. Pour some dip, full strength, into a pliable plastic dish. Completely immerse the coin in the liquid. Do not leave the coin in the liquid longer than a few seconds. Immediately rinse the coin thoroughly under running cold water. Pat (do not rub) the coin dry with a soft, absorbent cloth—a terrycloth towel is ideal. Holding the coin in your fingers and using a cotton swab to apply the dip may result in uneven cleaning. For copper coins use a diluted mixture of half dip and half cold water. Always make sure that your coins are thoroughly dry and at room temperature before storing. Practice cleaning processes with low-value coins—so if you do something wrong you will not suffer a monetary loss.

It is sometimes desirable on circulated coins to remove the light film of oxidation that sometimes forms on copper. A gentle rubbing with a soft cloth lightly treated with a commercial liquid product called "Care" will usually accomplish this task. Tape, glue, flecks of paint, and other substances found on coin surfaces usually will come off with the application of acetone, a solvent which is available at drug stores. Care must be taken to use acetone, coin dip, and other such solutions in a well ventilated area to prevent inhalation of harmful vapors.

Repeated cleaning of any coin will dull its surface over a period of time. For this reason, many advanced collectors prefer to have their coins with a light degree of toning—such as is normally acquired by the surface of a coin over a period of many years. The newcomer to the hobby, however, invariably thinks that "brilliant" equals "better," and wants his coins as bright as possible!

No discussion of cleaning would be complete without mentioning what dealers refer to as "treating" and "processing." This is something that no ethical dealer will do. Certain unscrupulous persons will take a lower-grade coin, an Extremely Fine or an AU piece for example, and attempt, sometimes very convincingly, to make it appear to be in "Uncirculated" or "Proof" condition. By brushing an AU coin against a wire wheel or other abrasive substance, sometimes a pseudo-lustre can be obtained. This will not fool the advanced collector (and you can be sure it will not fool the dealer you try to sell it to when you try to sell your coins!), but it will fool many beginners. A common trick is to take, for instance, an EF coin that is worth $10 and try to make it into an "Uncirculated" that would normally be worth $30. The trap is set when this newly-created "Uncirculated" is offered at a "bargain" price of just $20. A collector gets it thinking he is making the buy of a lifetime. Of course, the coin is only worth $10 or perhaps not even that considering that the surface has been treated. The best defense in this regard is to know your dealer. If in doubt, check with other numismatists for references. Remember also that the most successful dealers are not necessarily those with the largest advertising budgets—and a big ad does not automatically imply that the dealer is either large or successful. Indeed, some of the most successful of all dealers operate quietly, successfully, and efficiently by selling coins privately or by means of catalogues with limited circulation to a highly selective list of advanced collectors and dealers.

Don't let grading scare you. Approach the subject carefully and deliberately and with a degree of study—and you should have none of the problems I had when I was a beginning collector many years ago. Be careful about grading when you are buying—and then you will have no trouble when the time comes to sell your coins. Some common sense and care, combined with the counsel of a trusted fellow collector or dealer, will insure your success. Happy grading—and collecting!

From Rare Coin Review *No. 19, January-February 1974.*

Our Changing Hobby

| By Q. David Bowers | 1973 |

In 1972 Q. David Bowers was asked to contribute some of his reminiscences for publication in connection with the 20th anniversary of Numismatic News, the well-known Iola, Wisconsin coin newspaper. The following article is adapted from those recollections and is used with the permission of Numismatic News.

Changing Times

My, how things have changed!

Sometimes when thinking over past years, the 1950s seem like only yesterday. But in other respects those years seem to be from ancient history—or ever prehistoric times—in terms of today's coin field.

My own interest in coins began in the early 1950s when I was a student in high school. Like many collectors do today, I did most of my coin buying through the mail. It was always a delight to pore through the pages of the three leading numismatic magazines of the time—*Numismatic News, The Numismatic Scrapbook Magazine,* and *The Numismatist*—to find out what the latest bargains were. Each of these was published monthly—which gives you an idea of the pace of coin activity at the time. Nowadays some coin prices change daily, and in the case of certain volatile issues (such as common date gold coins), even hourly! Such things were unheard of 20 years ago, back in 1953.

Collecting Lincoln and Indian Cents

I started collecting as many collectors do: by looking through coins found in circulation. Today the chances of finding something rare—or even finding something *old* (but not rare)—in circulation are minimal.

Years ago the chances weren't great either, but they were infinitely better than they are now.

It was with disbelief I listened to a friend, Bonnie Tekstra, tell me recently she had visited a leading California tourist attraction and found a concessionaire doing a lively business selling "rare" Wheat Ears Reverse Lincoln cents (dated before 1959) at a premium. "These are a good investment," the vendor had assured her!

Twenty years ago things were vastly different. It was theoretically possible to fill a complete Lincoln cent set from circulation, although finding a 1909-S V.D.B. cent would have been a real accomplishment. Of course, if you couldn't find one in circulation you could always buy one from a coin dealer for about $10—or, if you wanted a Brilliant Uncirculated specimen, for about $15 to $20. By way of contrast, I mention that a Brilliant Uncirculated specimen would cost about $200 today.

Twenty years ago Indian cents were becoming quite rare in circulation. If you looked through a bag of 1,000 assorted cents you might find only one or two or three of the Indian type. You would, however, find quite a few 1909 V.D.B. cents (from the Philadelphia Mint)—and probably after a while you would do what I did: rather than accumulate large quantities of these common issues you would spend them again! You might be tempted to save, for instance, any Lincoln cent with a mintmark dated prior to 1915, but after a while you would tire of accumulating a lot of 1912-D, 1913-D and S, and other such issues which would never be worth anything—or would they?

A Young Collector's Good Fortune

I lived in the small Pennsylvania town of Forty Fort, a residential community situated on the banks of the Susquehanna River in the Wyoming Valley. One of my main collecting sources was the Forty Fort State Bank. At that time coin collectors were not considered to be a nuisance by banks—at least not by this very friendly bank. My interest in coins was welcomed, and tellers were more than happy to keep exchanging rolls of coins with me so I could find dates of interest. I remember that one single afternoon I had the good fortune to be able to put together a complete set of Liberty Walking half dollars from 1916 through 1947, with all dates and mints represented. This was done simply by looking through bank-wrapped rolls of half dollars until all were found! No, I didn't bother to save any extra 1921 half dollars or 1938-Ds. I was collecting; not investing or dealing. During that time there were also numerous Barber half dollars to be seen.

Around this time I thought it would be interesting to put together a set of Indian cents in Proof condition. The first coin I ever bought through the mail came from Copley Coin Company (Maurice M. Gould and Frank Washburn) of Boston, Massachusetts. It was a glittering Proof 1859 Indian cent which cost me all of $11. When it arrived in the mail I did not know whether it was a choice Proof or not, for I had never seen another Proof Indian cent! All I knew was it looked really beautiful to me, and I was happy to own it. Later, as I gained experience, I found it was indeed an exceptional Proof. By way of comparison I might mention that my present firm recently advertised a comparable 1859 Proof for $795—and sold it right away. My, how things have changed! Actually $11 was a high price for a Proof Indian cent back then. Commoner dates such as those in the 1880s and 1890s cost about $3 to $4 each. Of course, this was "expensive" to me at the time, for I was a high school student and I had a very limited budget.

Early Coin Dealing Experiences

Coin dealing was much less formal 20 years ago than it is now. In 1955, when I held my first bourse table at the American Numismatic Association's annual convention, I was still a high school student, and my credentials as a coin dealer consisted of a year or two of experience conducting a small part-time business by mail—with no complaints by customers having been registered to *The Numismatist* or to *The Numismatic Scrapbook Magazine*—the two places I did most of my advertising. In any event, my application for a table was readily accepted, and the first ANA convention was a really exciting event for me.

The scene of the ANA show that year was the Fontenelle Hotel in Omaha, Nebraska. The highlight of the convention for me was the purchase at $510 (a fraction of its value today) of an 1867 With Rays Proof Shield nickel. This coin, purchased at the convention auction held by Bebee's, was a record price at the time—and a number of people thought I was very silly for paying such a "high" price. However, one convention visitor, O.L. Harvey (who has since passed away) thought differently—and I accepted his offer of a modest profit over the price I paid.

I will never forget the kindnesses shown to me by the then old-timers in the trade. B. Max Mehl of Fort Worth, Texas made it a point to send me nice letters about my early catalogues—and letters coming from heaven couldn't have made a greater impact on my young and impressionable mind! I once mentioned to veteran dealer Abe Kosoff I could obtain several bags of mint condition scarce date silver dollars in a transaction which would amount to about $15,000. I was deeply impressed with his confidence in me when he wrote out a check for $15,000 on the spot and gave it to me in advance! $15,000 was more money than I had ever seen at one time!

When reminiscing about the "good old days" it is important to remember values were much different from what they are today. Perhaps to make $15,000 sound as impressive as it was then, I should compare it to $150,000 or perhaps even twice that today. At the aforementioned 1955 ANA convention, dealer Aubrey Bebee paid a record price—$200—for a prooflike Brilliant Uncirculated 1796 quarter. Not much more than a decade earlier—in 1941 to be exact—dealer B. Max Mehl sold one of America's greatest collections, the holdings of W.F. Dunham, at auction for a total of $83,364.08. This collection, containing an 1822 half eagle, 1804 silver dollar, and just about every other United States rarity, was a numismatic landmark; a sensation. And yet the total amount realized back in 1941—the previously mentioned $83,000 plus figure—would not equal the sales we achieve over a period of two or three weeks from a typical issue of the *Rare Coin Review*. So, everything has its own perspective.

In the 1950s, dealing was on a more unhurried basis. It was possible for a dealer to keep up with his numismatic reading. With only three leading publications to receive in the mail and with these publications being issued only once a month, it was no problem to keep abreast of the latest news. Today I am lucky if I have a chance to read 20% of the publications I receive—and to read them all would require doing nothing else but!

Unfortunately, it is no longer possible for me to personally know all of the dealers in America, for there are thousands of them now. Coin collecting, a leisurely hobby conducted by a close-knit group of collectors and dealers in the 1950s, has become a thriving industry today. Perhaps this is most poignantly stated by noting that shares of the Franklin Mint, an organization formed by a coin collector (with the original stock issue being largely sold to numismatists), achieved the exalted status one day last year of being number one on the New York Stock Exchange's most active list!

When I think back to the 1950s, I am proud to have been a part of coins for two decades and to have seen the remarkable change and growth in the coin market occur. I know dealers whose experiences ex-

tend back to times earlier than mine must feel an even greater senti-
ment in this regard.

Coin Pricing and Grading

Back in the 1950s coin prices were obtainable from two main
reference books: the *Guide Book of United States Coins* (which is still
being published and which is now in its 26th edition) and the *Standard
Catalogue of United States Coins* (which ceased publication in 1957).
Prices were much lower then—so grading was not such an important
consideration. If a given date of Indian cent was worth $1.50 in Uncir-
culated grade and perhaps 10 cents to 15 cents in Extremely Fine grade,
no one worried much about a distinction between, say, Very Fine and
Extremely Fine.

The "official grading policy" of *Numismatic News* (as stated in the
January 5, 1953 issue) points this out. There really wasn't much of a difference between, for instance, Extremely Fine and AU: "Extremely Fine
and About Uncirculated—amount to one and the same grade. This
grade of coin represents one which has seen little or no wear. Should
contain some mint lustre and may have been Uncirculated except for
the fact it contains mint scratches, dull spots, etc., due to careless handling." The next grade down the line was Fine. There was no mention
of Very Fine at all!

Today values are much higher, and minute distinctions in grading are
often made. If a coin catalogues $100 in Very Fine grade, $200 in Extremely Fine grade, and $500 in Uncirculated grade, then it is very im-
portant to have such distinctions as VF-EF and other split conditions
and grading fine points. Often a very small difference in grade can
mean a very big difference in value!

The Changing Ways of Collecting

Another thing which has changed over the years has been the attitude
toward the cleaning of coins. Years ago most people preferred Uncirculated coins to have light toning. Indeed, most museums and old-timers
still do. However, newcomers to the hobby have been trained to think
"brilliant" equals "quality" and "brilliant is best," so they often want
their coins to be brilliant—or else! Not helping matters are the profu-
sion of pastes, cleaners, solutions, etc., advertised to make your coins
"worth more."

The very ways of collecting have changed as well since the 1950s.
Time was when every collector aspired to have one of each date and

mintmark of the different 20th-century series. Visit a collector and he would show you his set of Lincoln cents, his set of Liberty nickels, his set of Mercury dimes, his set of Standing Liberty quarters, his sets of the three Barber denominations, and so on right down the line.

This collecting was not as ostentatious as it might seem now—for in an era in which an Uncirculated 1909-S V.D.B. cent cost $15 or $20, a Proof 1859 Indian cent $11, and that great silver dollar rarity, the Proof 1895, all of $250 or $300, a very large and impressive collection could be gathered together for just a fraction of what it would cost today. Indeed, it might cost more today to put together a set of Uncirculated and Proof nickels from 1866 to date than it would have cost to put together complete sets of everything I just mentioned 20 years ago!

On the same subject, I read with interest the other day that an 1894-S dime sold in the range of $50,000. I remember paying in 1957 the then-stunning price of $4,750 for a comparable piece. This news was so exciting at the time that it was the object of hundreds of newspaper articles all over the United States. The result was that countless thousands of letters and postcards descended upon me from all directions! "I have an 1894 dime, but without an S," or "I have a dime that is even older than your 1894-S; mine is dated 1893," were typical messages to me! I later appeared on the NBC *Today* show as a result of this purchase.

Today, collecting coins by types has taken the place, at least partially, of collecting by dates and mints. For a reasonable sum a numismatist can assemble a truly beautiful collection of coins and can own such interesting early pieces as half cents, large cents, nickel and silver three-cent pieces, and so on—without having to collect them by dates and mintmarks. In today's era, with a tremendously expanded number of collectors competing for the same number of coins, this collecting by type makes sense from several viewpoints. I am proud to recall Jim Ruddy and I "saw the handwriting on the wall" years ago and were among the first dealers to encourage collectors and investors to buy coins by design types. My own articles on type coin investment, which first appeared several years ago in the *Forecaster* investment newsletter and my earlier writings on the same subject for the *Empire Investors Report*, have made tremendous amounts of money for readers who read the articles and followed the recommendations given.

1953 to 1973
Investment has been a major reason to collect coins in recent years.

In the 1950s investment was a popular appeal of coins—but it was taken for granted. Today, investment is a specific activity per se—and many people assemble coin sets for investment alone. I interject at this point the observation that many things—some good and others bad—are perpetrated in the name of "coin investment." I believe coins have been and will continue to be excellent investments if you buy wisely and seek counsel from established professional dealers. However, this doesn't mean every coin is automatically a "good investment," any more than any rectangular piece of printed paper is automatically a blue chip stock certificate! Unfortunately, many "investment services" are operated by persons with very little knowledge or experience in the field of professional numismatics.

In the early 1950s the expectation was if you collected coins carefully and wisely you could sell your holdings for a nice profit—assuming you held them for a few years or longer. This almost always turned out to be the case. When coin collecting became extremely popular in the early 1960s, many astute persons looked at old coin prices and found out what a wonderful investment coins had been—and this spurred interest to still new heights.

Let us compare today with 20 years ago. Back then you could not be in a hurry about coin collecting. You could order coins from your monthly copy of *Numismatic News, The Numismatic Scrapbook Magazine,* or *The Numismatist.* Chances were there would have been no local coin club in your area unless you lived in a very large city. Chances were also excellent there would be no local coin shop. In fact, if you were a collector back then it might have been difficult for you to find another collector in your area.

On the plus side of the ledger, chances were good that if you went to a bank to ask for coins to look through from circulation, you would be welcomed with open arms—and, equally excellent, was the chance of finding something scarce. However, on the minus side of the ledger, those scarce items would not be worth much. In fact, among Mercury dimes, you might not even bother saving duplicates of any pieces other than 1916-D, 1921, 1921-D, and 1942/1. There are many, many coins cataloguing from $5 to $10 now which I remember spending then. Possibly that is why they are now commanding a premium.

Collectors were very friendly and helpful back then—and I like to think this is one aspect of numismatics which has not changed over the years! My youthful enthusiasm was nurtured by Robert Rusbar, Edmund Karmilowicz, and George Williams, and without their influence I probably would never have become a collector and then a dealer. George

Williams introduced me to the Wilkes-Barre Coin Club and tactfully advised me on the right and wrong ways to become popular (a dealer should only bid on an item at the club auction if a collector shows no interest, he advised, for example).

Back in the the early 1950s, if you wanted to order 100 Proof sets, or 1,000 Proof sets, from the Mint, that was just fine. In fact, I recall reading a letter from James, Incorporated (rare coin dealers of Louisville, Kentucky) which they received from the Mint; a letter thanking them profusely for their especially large order for Proof sets in 1951! Today the Mint restricts orders and would probably reject immediately any request for thousands of sets. Likewise, I remember writing to the Mint once and being told they did indeed have some leftover Proof sets of an earlier year and, of course, they would be happy to sel! them to me for the issue price! All this seems rather strange now!

At the same time, the new commemorative issues in the Washington-Carver series were "laying an egg" so far as sales were concerned. Few collectors wanted them.

As I write this now, the past seems unrealistic to me in many regards, and perhaps it seems even more unrealistic to you! It is almost as though a collector of that time was walking through fields carpeted with diamonds, but was too lazy to pick them up! Actually, however, everything has its own context—and in the early 1950s who was to know what the future would bring? Perhaps someone reading a 1973 coin catalogue 20 years from now will marvel at all of the incredible bargains! I am sure there are many coins selling for $5 to $10 now which will be worth 10 to 20 times that sum 20 years from now. This is well to remember when analyzing what happened 20 years ago.

Sometimes it is wistful to think of the past. It has been fun reminiscing with you. But we don't live in the past; we live in the present—and ahead of us lies the future. In a way it is fun to be a part of the present. Not for a moment do I wish I were back years ago. My 1859 Proof Indian cent was fun to own at the time, but from a dealer's viewpoint I would have a hard time selling it if I had asked $17 or $18 for it—so everything comes out even in the long run. Everything is relative.

At this point let me express the hope that you and I will both be around 20 years from now. Then we can talk about the "good old days" of 1973 and of all the bargains! Then our other friends of 1993 will say, "I only wish I could have lived way back then!"

But in 1993 we will have still newer things to look forward to, I am sure. I'll see you then!

From Rare Coin Review No. 17, Spring 1973.

Diversions

These interesting "definitions" by Fred Allen (memorable as one of the greatest radio comedians years ago) and "Lemuel Q. Stoopnagle" were furnished to us by the Vestal Press in New York—for your possible amusement.

ALIBIOGRAPHY. Life story of a guy who didn't make good.

ARCTICULATION. The eskimo language as it should be spoken.

AUTHORWRITIS. Writer's cramp.

CONCUBEEN. An old concubine.

GIRIFFRAFFE. A long-neck animal from the wrong side of the jungle.

DEBUTANTRUM. A society girl in a fit.

PILLFER. To steal from a doctor.

MA'AMOTH. A great big lady elephant of long ago.

MALTIMILLIONAIRE. A wealthy brewer.

SPLITIGATION. The proceeds of a lawsuit divided between the lawyers.

WRENOVATION. Readying a bird house for a new occupant.

YESTIMATE. To guess the number of affirmative votes.

Strange But True

JEFFERSON NICKELS would be better described as Jefferson *coppers,* for the alloy of most issues is three-quarters copper and just one-quarter nickel!

THE 1900 LAFAYETTE COMMEMORATIVE silver dollar, bearing the date 1900, was actually *prestruck* in 1899! Similarly, 1984-W (for West Point) Olympic $10 pieces were prestruck beginning in September 1983, 1976 bicentennial coins were prestruck beginning in 1975, and so on. While *restrikes* are often discussed, *prestrikes* are rarely mentioned in numisimatic literature.

THE TOTAL REALIZATION of all auctions held by noted dealer B.

Max Mehl during his illustrious career, plus the total realization of all auctions held by Henry Chapman and S. Hudson Chapman during their illustrious careers does not come close to equaling the $12.4 million realized by our *single auction sale* of the Louis Eliasberg Collection of United States gold coins held over a period of *just three days* in November 1982!

HENRY CHAPMAN, the famous professional numismatist, was well known for his personal *stamp* collection!

CINCINNATI COMMEMORATIVE half dollars issued in 1936 "to commemorate the 50th anniversary of Cincinnati as a center of music" actually observed an event that never took place. To this day, numismatists have not been able to determine what anniversary was being celebrated, nor have they learned of any significant musical happening that occurred in Cincinnati in 1886, 50 years before 1936!

THE FIRST BRANCH MINT COINS may have been 1837 *large cents* struck at New Orleans to test certain equipment there. These pieces bore no mintmark designation, nor were any trial strikings apparently saved.

Eternity

A friend recently told us of an interesting definition for the word "eternity." Actually, if it does not precisely define eternity it comes mighty close! His definition:

Imagine a block of granite measuring one mile on each side. Once every thousand years a sparrow lands on top of the block of granite, then quickly flies off again. The time needed for the granite block to wear down to nothing because of the contact with the bird's feet is eternity.

Travel Guide

One of our Texas readers, Cheri Kay Lemons, an airline executive who has been in the travel industry for most of her adult life, sent us a clipping the other day, original source not indicated, which gave the "true meaning" of words sometimes seen in travel brochures. Since many *Rare Coin Review* readers do indeed travel, if not for coins then at least for vacation purposes, and since we like to be as helpful as possible, the following translations are given for your edification!

Standard: Substandard.

Deluxe: Standard.

Superior: Free shower cap.

Quaint: Run-down.
Aristocratic: Hasn't been renovated.
Off the Beaten Path: Few want to come here.
Old-World Charm: No bath.
Tropical: Rainy.
Motorcoach: Bus.
Deluxe Motorcoach: Bus with clean windows.
Options Galore: Nothing included.
Secluded Hideaway: Impossible to get to.
Explore on Your Own: Pay for it yourself.
Playground of the Stars: George Snodgrass spent a night here in 1948.
Airy: No air conditioning.
Brisk: Freezing.
Gentle Breezes: Gale-force winds.
All the Amenities: Shoe-wiping cloth.
Sun-Drenched: Arid wasteland.
Leisurely Transfer: Tedious bus ride.
Knowledgeable Trip Hosts: They've read the brochure.
Nominal Charge: Outrageous charge.
Tipping not necessary: Unless you want good service.
And while we're at it, we'll throw in a few numismatic definitions (which we've made up ourselves):
Mint State: Pennsylvania, California, or Colorado.
Buffalo Nickel: Five-cent piece made in upstate New York somewhere near Niagara Falls.
Medium Date: An evening with a fortune teller.
Washington Quarters: Valley Forge.
Type Set: Something printers do.
Pine Tree Shilling: Hustling Christmas trees.
Plain Edge: The Mississippi River.
High Relief: The thrill of mountain climbing.
Philadelphia Mint: A piece of candy made in the City of Brotherly Love.

From Rare Coin Review *No. 52, June-September 1984.*

An 1891 View of Coinage

By Q. David Bowers   1983

Nowadays the average American citizen is used to a wide variety of coinage. The designs of the Lincoln cent, Jefferson nickel, Roosevelt dime, Washington quarter, Kennedy half dollar, and the late lamented Anthony dollar all differ widely from each other. And, the 1982 Washington commemorative half dollar adds a bit of spice to the current coinage scene as do the anticipated Olympics pieces.

Back in 1891 the situation was far different. American silver commemorative coins had not yet been invented and silver pieces in circulation were mostly of the Liberty Seated design. The dime, quarter, and half dollar essentially featured the same motif. And, attractive as the Morgan silver dollar is to numismatists today, during the period of its issue the design was widely criticized.

The July 9, 1891 issue of *The Youth's Companion* featured an article on the subject of, "Our Proposed New Coinage," excerpts of which are given herewith:

> One of the bills passed in the last Congress instructed the director of the United States Mint to procure new designs for our silver coins. It was intended to change the designs on both sides of the silver dollar, and on the face of the small silver pieces.

> The director of the Mint, in his circular to the artists of the country, inviting them to compete, offered a prize of $500 for each design accepted. The leading designers and sculptors of the United States considered the amount of the prize too small, and declined to compete. They wished, too, to have the designs ordered, then paid for whether they were accepted or not.

When the competing designs submitted by other artists were opened on the first of June the committee found none better than the designs now in use on our coin. All were therefore rejected, and, therefore, we shall not have our new coinage until another more successful trial has been made. This may possibly not be for a year or more: for the artists who objected to the Mint director's proposition asked also for a longer time in which to prepare their drawings.

One great difficulty in the way of the artists is the limited variety in the designs which can be used for national coins. The coinage is not like government paper money and postage stamps, on which in this country are usually printed the pictures of eminent dead statesmen or generals.

Since the foundation of the government, practically only two designs have been used for the face of either gold or silver coins. One is the head of the allegorical Goddess of Liberty; the other is the full figure of Liberty seated with a shield in her hand.

Both of these designs are now in use, the first on the silver dollar and the second on the half dollar and minor silver coins.

There have been surprisingly few alterations, even in these designs. The design on half dollars and small silver has not been changed since 1837 when it was substituted for the simple head of Liberty.

The dollars, however, have been altered four or five times, changing from the head of Liberty with no cap and loose flowing hair, in the coinage of 1794 and 1795, to the same full figure as our half dollars now bear; and then again, 13 years ago, to the Greek face on the present dollar. [Editorial note: the actual portrait used was of Miss Anna Williams, a Philadelphia schoolteacher.]

The reverse side has always borne the eagle, but in a great variety of postures, sometimes flying forward through the air, sometimes simply spreading its wings and bearing the Union shield on its breast.

It is not easy to plan out a really original design with so limited a field for ideas. Not one of the coinage designs in our history has been entirely satisfactory; yet repeated experiments, and especially the experience of this year's competitive work, show how difficult it is to improve upon what we already have. . . .

The United States has the reputation of leading the world in the work of fine engraving. [Editor's note: this is in reference to the beautiful currency issued by the United States government during the period.] Many authorities believe that we shall gain an equally high rank in artistic ingenuity and originality [once new coinage designs are formulated].

As numismatists know, the Morgan dollar was not changed. The design was kept in use until 1921. Liberty Seated coins were changed the following year, 1892, when Charles Barber's Liberty Head design, now known as the Barber coinage, first made its appearance. The Barber coins were unenthusiastically received, and in 1895 a nationwide design competition for a new coinage was instituted. Nothing came of it, and change awaited the appearance of the beautiful Mercury dime, Standing Liberty quarter, Liberty Walking half dollar in 1916, and the Peace dollar in 1921.

From Rare Coin Review No. 48, June-July 1983.

The Passing of the Torch

By Q. David Bowers   1983

The old order changes, and, as difficult as it may be, we all must grow accustomed to the absence of certain individuals who were close or important to us. It seems that during the past year, the numismatic field has had more than its rightful share of deaths. Last summer the passing of Amon Carter, Jr., the well-known Fort Worth, Texas numismatist, came as a shock. Amon, the very picture of bustling activity in a hundred different areas that interested him, was hardly the candidate for leaving the scene. But, an unpredicted heart attack did its work, in this case instantly.

I first met Amon many years ago, probably in 1954 or 1955. I was attending a coin convention, and we happened to meet in an elevator. He apparently recognized me from a catalogue or advertisement because he introduced himself. I had heard of him by reputation but had not had the pleasure of making his acquaintance.

"Have you ever seen a $10,000 bill?," he asked. Well, I hadn't, and I told him so. "Have you ever seen *seven* $10,000 bills?" Of course, I hadn't. Whereupon he withdrew from his coat pocket seven pieces of currency, each of this awesome $10,000 denomination. What a thrill it was to a budding numismatist still in his teens, a person to whom even a $500 or $1,000 bill would be a novelty, to see such an array!

Lest the reader think this display was ostentatious or done with "conspicuous consumption" in mind, let me hasten to say this was not the case. Amon was a low-key person, who despite his status as one of America's wealthiest individuals, was a "regular" fellow. He was most comfortable in his shirtsleeves, smoking a cigar, and admiring someone else's holdings, perhaps a limp piece of currency, not of great value, but with an interesting geographical location or imprint. While he personally possessed at one time or another many major rarities, including an 1822 half eagle (now in the Smithsonian Institution), an 1885 trade dollar, a set of 1879-1880 $4 Stellas, and others, still he enjoyed working with quantities of circulated pieces of relatively low value. I remember during one visit to his office he showed me huge quantities of circulated Canadian nickels which he was searching through in order to find scarce dates. Other times he would order from banking friends thousands of new $1 bills in order to sort through them and find interesting serial numbers, a note with all sevens, for example.

His interest was inherited from his father, who first was bitten by the numismatic "bug" when B. Max Mehl gave him an 1879 quarter eagle as a gift. His interest aroused, Amon Carter, Sr. asked what other 1879 coins could be purchased. Soon he owned a rare 1879 $4 piece, the prelude to what eventually became one of America's most important numismatic holdings. Mehl used to conduct sales by mail bids rather than by public auction, and there were always some pieces which either received no bids or bids which the seller did not consider to be satisfactory. On a number of occasions Carter was contacted, and he would buy in one fell swoop the remainders. His son, Amon, Jr., showed me several boxes full of such items, left intact from many decades earlier!

When I was just beginning to attend coin shows in the 1950s, Amon Carter, Jr. once brought his 1804 silver dollar, a beautiful specimen of what is perhaps America's most famous rarity, and put it in my showcase. I asked him why he did this, and he said it would bring some attention my way, something I could use. I was concerned about the extreme value of the coin, and Amon told me that was his responsibility, not mine, and he wasn't worried about it.

Amon maintained his office in the building of the Fort Worth *Star-Telegram,* a newspaper which he owned. His office reminded me of the den of an antiquarian or hobbyist. Unlike many "captains of industry" who might maintain modern facilities with scarcely a paperclip out of order, Amon's office was meant to be lived in, and it was. Interesting artifacts of the past, including many shovels from ground-breaking ceremonies in which he had been involved, decorated the room. A more interesting place could not be imagined.

During one visit to his office he excused himself from our conversation to take a telephone call from a Florida museum owner who was seeking some capital to finance an undersea treasure hunt. An hour later Amon hung up the telephone. His words were something like, "Well, I've been involved in all sorts of other financial ventures, so why not sunken treasure as well?" How he made out with his investment, I don't know, but I doubt if it made much difference. He did it for the fun involved.

In his home town, he established a museum of western art which today is perhaps the most important in its field. Several years ago it was announced that an incomparable collection of western photographs, the former property of Fred and Jo Mazzula, had been acquired intact, a treasure trove of tens of thousands of images. Being interested in western history, I contacted Amon at the time to see if it would be possible to locate any pictures of Cripple Creek or Victor, Colorado, whose gold mining history I find particularly fascinating. Amon, in effect, told me that any time I wanted to come to Fort Worth, I could have the "run" of the collection, even though it had not yet been sorted.

In addition to the *Star-Telegram*, Amon Carter's financial interests included Gulf Oil, American Airlines, and many other investments. It was recounted that once Amon was hurrying to make a connection, but the American Airlines plane had pulled away from the gate just moments before. Flashing his board of directors' card, he said, "Well, bring it back!" and the plane was brought back to the gate. Again, to appreciate this incident one has to know Amon. Far from being done in an ostentatious manner, the people involved had a good laugh concerning the situation, for it was done in fun.

Amon was generous. His beneficiaries included just about anyone he could help, including the American Numismatic Association, numismatists engaged with research (particularly in the field of paper money, his main interest), and in numerous other areas, nearly all of which were unpublicized.

With Amon's passing, all who knew him lost a friend with a Texas-size heart.

Then, early in the present year, came the untimely death of Richard Picker, the well-known New York numismatist who specialized in colonials and other early American issues. There are coin dealers and there are coin dealers; they come in all shapes, sizes, and degrees of competence. Dick was among the finest, right in the front row. Dick was what every dealer hopes to be, or at least *should* hope to be. Not only was he admired by his clients, he really knew his field. Die varieties of Connecticut, Vermont, Massachusetts, New Jersey, and other early colonial pieces were second nature to him. And, knowledge concerning how rare they are in given conditions, pricing and availability, and other aspects was always ready to be shared.

When the present writer produced *The History of United States Coinage As Illustrated by the Garrett Collection,* Dick Picker proofread the colonial section and gave many valuable suggestions. Likewise, in instances more numerous than can be remembered, Dick provided information concerning pedigrees, history, rarity, authenticity, or another facet of coins being offered by my firm for private sale or public auction. I always asked if we could use his name as a credit, and, not seeking publicity, he always demurred.

In October 1982, when I was in New York City for a week prior to the United States Gold Coin Collection (the collection formed by Louis Eliasberg), I spent an enjoyable hour or two talking with Dick, who had come to view the coins being offered by us for the New York Public Library Collection auction being held at the same time. Dick told how he was retiring from the business but how he enjoyed the people so much that he would always be in close contact. I told him that the field of buying and selling early American coins would not be the same without him. He would be missed. "You can call me anytime I can help with anything," was his reply. He did want to stay involved, not in the trade, but with new discoveries and research. And then a few weeks later came word of his illness. And then, later, his death.

When someone admired and close to you dies, the emotions are mixed. There is, of course, a sense of loss, but also anger. Why did this happen? Did it have to happen? There is the sense of wanting to do something, but nothing can be done. A telephone call to Margo Russell, editor of *Coin World,* suggested that a special tribute to Dick Picker be published. But, this had already been thought of. Within a few weeks, Eric P. Newman, one of Dick's closest friends, contacted me for a written contribution. If Dick had been asked whether he would have liked such a tribute, he probably in his modesty would have declined.

I will miss Dick. For many years we have shared information, comments, his heartbreak when coins were stolen at the ANA convention in Washington in 1971 (and the unfortunate legal altercation to determine the responsibility which ensued), and other matters all brought us very close. Dick will always be remembered and admired by those who knew him.

Then in March came the news of the death of Abe Kosoff. Known as the "dean of American numismatists" for many years, Abe—retired from his role as a professional—provided much advice and counsel to the American Numismatic Association, dealers, and friends.

With Abner Kreisberg he ran the Numismatic Gallery, which was especially prominent in the decade 1944-1954. Handled were many outstanding properties, including the F.C.C. Boyd Collection, which was sold anonymously as The World's Greatest Collection (for Boyd eschewed publicity). The collection of movie star Adolphe Menjou, the large cents of Oscar Pearl, the pattern and other coins of Michael Higgy (the sale of which Abe Kosoff was fond of crediting as the main impetus to the "modern coin market" of the 1940s), and other holdings attracted nationwide attention. In later years he and Abner Kreisberg went their own ways, with each achieving a great measure of individual success. The James O. Sloss, Thomas Melish, Edwin Hydeman, and other auctions held during the 1950s and 1960s are remembered today by specialists and collectors of numismatic literature.

A long-term close personal friendship with Dr. J. Hewitt Judd resulted in the publication over 20 years ago of Dr. Judd's book, U.S. Patterns, which contained much of Abe's research. After that time, year by year, Abe updated the prices and information. Not until the seventh edition did Abe put his name upon the cover, a long overdue recognition. As publisher of the book in recent editions, I enjoyed working with Abe each time a new revision was released. He learned the art of management well and never second-guessed the activities of our firm. When a problem came up, as they did occasionally with such a complex publishing project, Abe always said something like, "Well, you work it out, and whatever you decide is fine with me."

In the mid-1950s, when I started attending coin shows and auctions, I was very impressed by those who had "gone before," the old-time numismatists, still living, who actually were there when many great things happened. It was a pleasure to know B. Max Mehl, who was a living legend in his own time. Morton and J.B. Stack, now also deceased, were always very friendly to me and took the time to answer what probably were tedious questions. James Kelly, Al Overton, Earl Parker, and other numismatic greats were thrilling to meet, to buy coins from, to talk with, and simply to know.

My memory is fuzzy concerning my first meeting with Abe Kosoff, but it was very early in my career. He asked me where I was from, and I related that my home was in northeastern Pennsylvania. It seemed that he had a friend who wanted to buy mint-sealed bags of silver dollars, which at that time could be ordered through banks for face value. Depending upon the area of the country you were in, you might get San Francisco coins, Philadelphia coins, or whatever. As Abe had ready access to West Coast sources with San Francisco coins, he wanted someone in the East to place an order in the hope of obtaining Philadelphia pieces. Although he knew nothing about my credit or capital, and had scarcely met me, he gave me a cashier's check for $15,000 and asked me to use it to buy some silver dollar bags. I could not quite understand why such a prominent numismatist would not have other sources or why he would place his trust in a youngster such as me, but I was flattered, did the best job I could for him and his client, and never forgot the situation.

Abe's career was not without its reversals, the primary one of which was the passing of his son, Steve, at the young age of 29. Steve, together with Mike Kliman (who maintains an active coin dealership today), owned Numismatic Enterprises, a firm which under the tutelage of Abe Kosoff was slated for prominence. Alas, that did not come to full fruit. I flew from New York to California to attend Steve's funeral and remember contemplating at the time how unjust the entire situation seemed to be. Why could he not have had a 50-year long career?

Sometimes when one pictures coin dealers, one thinks they eat, sleep, and breathe coins. Perhaps in some cases this is true. But, in many other instances numismatists have well-rounded lives with many varied activities. When Abe Kosoff lived in Encino, California prior to his move to Palm Springs years ago, he invited me for lunch to his country club. While he and I were talking about coins, numerous other club members, most of whom probably didn't know the difference between a coin and a stamp, were addressing him as "president." I came to find that he was not only president of his country club, but one of the most popular officers the organization had ever elected. Likewise, he was involved in many other activities.

A number of years ago, Abe Kosoff was responsible for the institution of the Founders' Award by the Professional Numismatists Guild. This award, the highest bestowed by this organization, was given to various individuals. Then the award committee thought about giving it to Abe himself. A discussion ensued as to whether Abe would refuse the award or whether it would be appropriate. But, something seemed wrong about not giving Abe, who founded the PNG, the highest award of the group, especially if he had no reason to expect it. So, the award was given. And, in view of Abe's recent death, I am sure that all PNG members are pleased that this recognition took place.

The Passing of the Torch

At a banquet of the Numismatic Association of Southern California in 1979 Abe Kosoff was the guest of honor. The subject was his 50th anniversary in the coin trade. Earlier in his active years his advertisements always proclaimed "Since 1929." Here it was, 1979, and in a "This is Your Life" situation (with most of the work done in advance by Margo Russell), prominent events in Abe's life were recounted. It was quite a sentimental occasion.

Among the several giant figures who passed from the numismatic scene during the past year, none looms larger than the memory of Dr. Vladimir Clain-Stefanelli, curator for many years of the Numismatic Division at the Smithsonian Institution. Under his capable direction, with the wonderful partnership of his wife, Elvira, the Smithsonian exhibit, which includes the former U.S. Mint Collection, went from a rather haphazard display to one of world prominence. To such landmark rarities as the unique 1849 $20, both die varieties of the 1877 $50 in gold, and other gems, were added many pieces, including the intact gold collection of Josiah K. Lilly, the famous Indianapolis pharmaceutical manufacturer whose holdings were acquired by a special congressional act about 15 years ago. The good that Dr. Stefanelli did will live beyond him, and visitors to the Smithsonian Institution who see the brilliantly conceived exhibit, which mixes education with rarity, will continue to pay tribute to his efforts.

Modesty was one of Dr. Stefanelli's characteristics. Whenever he called or wrote—to have us appraise a 1913 Liberty Head nickel, an 1855 Kellogg $50, or for any of many different reasons over the years—he always unnecessarily prefaced his comments with an apology for intruding on our time, something we always found amusing, for we would have dropped anything else anyway just to be of help!

Recent decades in numismatics have seen many changes, and certainly one of the better changes has been the implementation of a simply superb exhibition at the Smithsonian Institution. The coins that belong to all of us at last are displayed the way they deserve to be. And, the exhibit is a fitting monument to the man who created it.

The families of Amon Carter, Dick Picker, Abe Kosoff, and Dr. Vladimir Clain-Stefanelli all know that in addition to the admiration *they* hold, a much wider circle exists in each instance countless thousands of numismatists who will never forget them.

From Rare Coin Review *No. 48, June-July 1983.*

Numismatic Politics

| By David L. Ganz | 1974 |

Writing about numismatics has given me a unique insight into coin collecting as a potential investment, a big business, and an important national lobby. Throughout a four-year stint as the Washington correspondent for *Numismatic News Weekly*, during four previous years as an editorial columnist for several coin periodicals, and currently, I have had the privilege of putting "under the glass" a variety of subject matter that falls within the penumbra of being numismatically related.

The most important thing that I have always tried to bear in mind in my writing is that I am a hobbyist, too. When researching a subject, or when even thinking about ideas for future articles, the question I generally ask is: "What would I like to read if I weren't going to be writing this?" Inevitably the result is much closer to what *you* really want to read.

Humor is also an important factor. In this business you've got to have it. Otherwise, the rejection slips get to you after a while. I gave up trying to be funny in my columns and articles a long while ago, but not before I got a letter from a publisher stating in no uncertain terms: "I am publishing your humorous article on making 'weeds' our new national currency, though I question its importance or value."

Now I try to limit my humorous comments to politics—usually in reference to political tokens or medals—because most politicians want to run for office in the worst way, and they usually do!

Politicians—when they're not running for office—can be fairly humorous people. At least that's the experience I've had in four years of chatting with them in their Capitol Hill offices. One senator, who for obvious reasons will remain nameless, was chatting with me in 1970 when an aide knocked on the door to his office and whispered to him that Cambodia had been invaded by American fighting troops. The senator paled visibly, turned to me, and gave me the sad news hours before the rest of the country would hear about it from Walter Cronkite. Then, brightening, he exclaimed: "Wait a minute—there's no problem. We're taking over Cambodia to make Martha Mitchell queen for a day!" Not terribly numismatic, but it shows that politicians have a sense of humor.

Undoubtedly the most frustrating events I have watched on Capitol Hill are the enacting of laws which are obviously needed but which are fairly unimportant so far as matters of state go. One example of this is the Hobby Protection Act, passed in 1973 by Congress, which prohibits the sale of unmarked coin reproductions and related items.

The bill was first introduced in 1969 by Rep. James A. McClure, but no action was taken. A second version was introduced the following session by Rep. Seymour Halpern, and when that didn't go anywhere, a "numismatic lobby" tried to take Washington by storm. Although this didn't result in any real action, it later caused the chairman of the appropriate committee to introduce a similar measure which he ordered hearings held on.

When the bill finally came up for a vote in the House, four and one-half years after McClure had first proposed it, he wasn't there anymore; he'd run for the Senate in the interim and was now on the other side of Capitol Hill where, presumably, he could help marshal forces for the bill.

An hour's debate preceded the vote on the Hobby Protection Act. As a member of the press gallery of the House of Representatives, I witnessed the debate from a unique vantage point. The highlight of the debate came when H.R. Gross asked why any debate on the non-controversial measure was needed. Why should Congress spend an hour's time to debate something that nobody would oppose? Gross then answered his own question by stating that Congress was debating the bill to give the appearance to the American people that the members were doing something—when plainly, he said, they were not!

Finally a motion was made to vote on the legislation, and the Speaker of the House called for the members to insert their plastic cards in the electronic voting device that quickly counts each member's vote. The gadget was installed to save time, but the day that the Hobby Protection Act was passed, it wasn't working.

The result was that the Clerk of the House had to call out each congressman's name, to which he had to answer "aye" or "nay," depending upon how he wanted to vote on the bill. This was done twice—in case an absent member returned. From my observation point in the gallery it was quite a spectacle.

Congressmen walked onto the House floor, expecting the plastic card voting apparatus to be functioning, saw that it wasn't, and began to complain to their colleagues about it. Soon 389 members of the House were all complaining at once! Adding to the din was the Clerk, who was shouting out names for each Congressman to respond to in turn.

The final result of the vote was 382 to 7, a rather overwhelming victory. But why did seven congressmen vote against it? The answer in one instance was apologetically explained to me later by a "nay" voter: he was outside when he heard the bells signifying a roll-call vote. He ran to the floor and asked a colleague what the vote was on. The collegue, who also was going to vote against the bill, said, "It's a bill to expand the power of the Federal Trade Commission; I am against it!"

The Hobby Protection Act does indeed expand the powers of the FTC to regulate the sale of replicas and reproductions that are not marked, but it hardly constitutes a substantive or oppressive expansion of general powers or a restriction of citizen's rights. Yet, as the congressman told me, "That's typical of what goes on here all the time!"

The United States Senate is far more of a club than is the House of Representatives, largely because the 100 Senate members are chummy with each other for long periods of time. Serving six-year terms is a great advantage for senators (unlike the House, where it seems as if you're running for office continually). A senator can "speak his conscience" for four years, and worry about getting re-elected during the last two years of his term.

Most of the members of the Senate speak their minds frequently.

Back to the Hobby Protection Act: it was introduced in the Senate and after some pressure it was brought up on the floor for a vote just as Congress was getting ready for its summer recess. There was a beef price freeze at the time, causing a critical beef shortage. James McClure, who had authored the original Hobby Protection Act when he was a representative in the House four years earlier, introduced an amendment to end the beef price freeze. The bill and its new amendment passed the Senate quickly. However, the House did not concur, and final passage of the measure was delayed until November 29th. So, Senator McClure, in effect, delayed his own bill!

Gold ownership by American citizens is another issue that had been tackled many times by Congress, though nothing substantive had yet been accomplished. During the 92nd and 93rd Congresses, the Senate twice passed measures calling for prompt ownership—restoring a right Americans lost in 1934. The House of Representatives, notoriously more conservative than the Senate in matters of finance, twice succeeded in killing the proposal, but not before gold ownership lost on a tied 161 to 161 vote on the floor of the House.

I was not in the galleries the day the House voted on gold ownership, having left Washington earlier to join the editorial staff of *Numismatic News Weekly*. However, there were plenty of other people in the galleries, including the staffs of several committees and interested congressmen and, apparently, also someone from investigative reporter Jack Anderson's column. The result: apparent irregularities in voting were reported, including other members voting a colleague's card in the electronic device, aides voting their bosses' card, and the like.

Earlier, the Senate had considered the gold ownership question, and an even stranger situation occurred. Senator Mark O. Hatfield, with whom I had recently spoken about the gold ownership question, decided to spearhead efforts to get not only gold ownership, but a gold bicentennial coin.

After failing to persuade the Senate Banking Subcommittee on Minting and Coinage, and the full committee in make-up session, Hatfield took his case to the Senate floor. Again, I was not present for the debate (and neither were more than 90 senators!), but my lack of attendance was more than made up—for minutes after the debate successfully ended I received a telephone call at my *Numismatic News* office in Iola, Wisconsin. I heard a familiar voice say, "David, this is Mark Hatfield speaking. We just had the strangest thing happen on the Senate floor. We won gold ownership on a four to three vote!"

As Senator Hatfield described it to me, he had joined forces with two other good friends, James McClure and Peter Dominick. The three of them matched wits against three other senators on the floor, Robert Taft, Jr., William Hathaway, and John Tower—all of whom opposed the measure.

"We decided to try to beat them on a voice vote—by outshouting them," Mark Hatfield continued, "but when John Tower asked for a vote, presiding officer James Abourezk voted with me to approve the gold ownership amendment four to three!"

Making the rounds to Senate and House offices is a ritual that only a fellow Washington reporter can appreciate. It's tiring, time-consuming, but it is important to maintain good relations with the members of Congress and their aides.

Sometimes an interview can be frustrating. For example, last November I had hoped to elicit some newsworthy comments from Senator William Hathaway of Maine, chairman of the ad hoc Banking Subcommittee on Minting and Coinage. In talking with him about the gold ownership situation I brought up every possible reason why Americans should be allowed to hold gold, and then I asked if he shared this view. I was hoping, of course, for a long and elaborate answer which would have become a page one news story. Senator Hathaway, with the terseness which has made many Maine "down-easters" legendary, simply said "Yes."

Covering the Treasury Department often has its frustrations. Some officials don't like to be quoted, and when they are, they will deny having said anything. Mint Director Mary Brooks isn't like that, however, and she usually speaks candidly and freely.

In one memorable meeting with Mrs. Brooks, I asked her about the possibility of striking a gold bicentennial coin. This was long before such an idea was popular. She not only liked the idea, but she thought generalized gold ownership ought to go along with it. I left the office an hour later with a scoop, returned home to Virginia to write it, and by the next morning was ready to call it in to *Numismatic News* when a Mint official called and requested that the story be killed. Gold had gone up $5 or $6 the day before, making the market quite volatile, and the Treasury was afraid that Brooks' comment might add speculative fuel to the fire. I honored the request, after consulting with my editors, but no before I solicited the promise to be allowed to break the story when the "time was right."

This turned out to be one of the few times that the Treasury forgot a promise—because it was less than six months later that I saw identical comments made in a rival publication, with attribution to Brooks. Quite frankly, I hit the roof! My frustration was compounded because I had been with Brooks when she made the remark a second time, had again checked to see if the news could be used, and was again respectfully refused. Such is life!

In June 1972 Brooks spoke to me about the possibility of having a White House ceremony for unveiling her pet project—a book about the presidents on American coins. I thought the idea was a good one from a public relations viewpoint, and I promptly set out to get the Washington Junior Coin Club included in the event. Brooks called on Tricia Nixon to help out, and we all had a fine party in the Rose Garden of the White House.

Working with Mary Brooks at the Mint has been both an interesting and an enjoyable experience. Also I have enjoyed my working relationship with James A. Conlon, director of the Bureau of Engraving and Printing.

In 1971 probably the most difficult task I had was to try to persuade the Bureau of Engraving and Printing that the young numismatists attending the annual convention of the American Numismatic Association (held that year in Washington) should be given a floor tour of the place where all of our nation's currency is manufactured. Normally, floor tours are forbidden at the security-conscious Bureau, but the juniors got what my friend Paul Whitnah called "a tour that money couldn't buy." Unfortunately, as some juniors later remarked, they weren't offered any samples!

That same year, with the help of former Mint Director Eva Adams, the juniors were treated to lunch in the East Conference Room of the Supreme Court of the United States, and to a special tour of the Smithsonian Institution. As one of the chief convention co-ordinators for the junior members, I am proud to have helped with a convention that will never be forgotten by these young numismatists—the collectors and dealers of the future.

If there is one thing that I enjoyed about my tenure in the nation's capital, it was living in the Washington area. Frankly, I consider Washington to be the most beautiful city in this country, because it belongs to all Americans. Many landmarks are commemorated on current money: the Lincoln Memorial (on the reverse of the Lincoln cent and the $5 bill), the Treasury Building (reverse of the $10 bill), the White House (reverse of the $20 bill), and the Capitol (reverse of the $50 bill), for instance. All Americans can share Washington. As a resident there, nothing gave me greater pride and pleasure than taking an out-of-town friend on a "grand tour" of my adopted city—a city that belonged to him or her just as much as to me.

In a way, that's what this article has done also—it has shown *you*, an out-of-town "friend," the Washington you may have heard about but may never have experienced: the politics of numismatics. I've enjoyed "showing" my special area of Washington to you, and I hope you've enjoyed reading about it.

From Rare Coin Review *No. 20, May-June 1974.*

David L. Ganz was Washington correspondent for Numismatic News Weekly *from*

November 1969 to May 1973.

His numismatic credits are many. Since 1965 he has had over 1,000 articles published, including nearly 50 full-length feature story presentations. His credit lines have appeared in nearly every numismatic publication and, to show his versatality, some non-numismatic ones as well (for example, Table Tennis Topics).

In 1974 Ganz enrolled at St. John's University in New York and earned a degree in law. He entered practice in New York City, achieving prominence as a numismatic lawyer. In 1985 he was elected to the Board of Governors of the ANA.

An 1870 Coin Auction

By Q. David Bowers   1983

I n January of 1983 the writer attended Papermania, a show held in Hartford, Connecticut, which featured "paper" items—posters, postcards, old books, magazines, and the like. While there were no numismatic exhibits in evidence, I knew as I began my perusal of the various aisles and dealers' exhibits there was bound to be something numismatically related, perhaps an advertisement for Ayer's Sarsaparilla or Ayer's Pills (numismatically remembered as advertisements which appear on encased postage stamps issued in 1862), or possibly some old obsolete currency (which, after all, are indeed paper items).

Breweriana, as the field is called—the study of items related to breweries—offered another possibility. Of all names prominently associated with American numismatics, Virgil Brand is one of the most prominent. Beginning his interest in 1889, he intensely absorbed himself in the field until his untimely death in 1926. Along the way he acquired *several hundred thousand* coins. Making all of this possible was the Brand Brewery, located in Illinois. Well, breweries like to advertise and at a given paper show one usually sees colorful posters, intended for display in taverns and saloons at the turn of the century, showing factories of Coors, Anheuser Busch, Centlivre, and others, some of which are remembered today but most of which have long since been forgotten. Was a poster ever made of the Brand Brewery? I didn't know. And I still don't know. However, if I locate one, chances are it will cost no more than an ordinary brewery poster, for few collectors of breweriana would know about its related numismatic significance. Such provides the thrill of the chase.

I had nearly completed my tour of the Papermania show when I spied what appeared to be a poster or broadside nonchalantly leaning against the wall behind a dealer's booth. The word "COINS" in the headline caught the corner of my eye and I sought a closer look. Obligingly the owner lifted it from its position and handed it to me. The price? $35. Big deal. It is bad form to ask the price of something at the outset, lest one appear to be too interested in an antique or paper item. Actually, one should practice the art of being nonchalant on such occasions!

In about three and one half seconds I just knew I had to have this poster. Indeed, I do not recall ever having had a 19th-century coin *poster* before, simply because the poster was not often used for advertising or, perhaps posters were used, but few have survived. Anyway, what I had in my hand was indeed a poster, and it advertised a coin auction sale.

To be specific, the headline told me that Thos. Birch & Son, located at 1110 Chestnut Street, which I knew to be in Philadelphia (but which was not stated on the poster), was to hold a sale of "Valuable Collection of Coins, Curiosities, etc." on Wednesday, Dec. 28, 1870 at 3:00 in the afternoon.

What I had in my hand was more than a poster, it was the auction catalogue! Probably the poster, printed on one side, was placed in store windows and on bulletin boards throughout the city prior to the event. The descriptions of the coins and other items were not extensive enough to have permitted bidding by mail. Rather, they simply offered an enticement to attend the actual event, which is precisely what posters are supposed to do!

Over a century ago, in 1870, numismatists often were intensely interested in other things as well, a situation which might not be all that bad if it were still true today. Actually, it is true today so far as certain individuals are concerned. Henry Spangenberger, for one, is not only a first-class numismatist but he frequently buys and sells printed material, posters and banners, and many other things from his Ohio premises. Gary Sturtridge, who presently serves as president of the Professional Numismatists Guild, has a lively business of buying and selling antique slot machines in addition to his very successful coin dealership. And, there are other examples.

Back in 1870 such situations were more the rule than the exception. A decade later the Chapman brothers, S. Hudson and Henry, who in 1870 were still wearing short pants, were to advertise themselves as "antiquaries," which, presumably, meant the same as "antiquarians," or dealers in antique objects. W. Elliot Woodward, the prominent rare coin dealer from Roxbury, Massachusetts, bought and sold fossils, Indian arrowheads, documents, and a host of other things in addition to numismatica. So, on Wednesday, December 28, 1870 it was not at all unusual for a coin sale to be larded with "curiosities," as the poster headline put it.

Fortunately, the poster in my possession was actually used, and its former owner noted in pencil certain of the prices realized. Some of the curiosities were indeed curious, as was the combining of diverse items within a single lot. For example, Lot 3 consisted of photographs of Charles Dickens and his wife, as well as billiard players, certainly an eclectic situation! Lot 7 offered, and I quote, "Battle of New Orleans, etc." Obviously the battle itself could not have been offered, so perhaps an engraving of it, a book, or some artifact was the subject.

Lot 11 consisted of "Coin Catalogues, 12 pamphlets." This was followed by Lot 12 consisting of "Introductory Lectures, 16 pamphlets." An introduction to what? It wasn't stated. The following offering, four pamphlets including the "Essay on Marriage," realized 60 cents.

So far there was nothing numismatic. Then came Lot 15 described as "Lot, Old U.S. Mint Dies, 7 pieces." Unfortunately, so far as this lot is concerned, this poster was not a catalogue so no further description was given. What type of dies were offered? No one knows. Our attendee at the sale marked in pencil the notation "Stopped" after that lot, rather than a realized price, indicating that the government must have found out about the offering and seized the specimens.

Lot 84 offered a quantity lot of "Washington portraits, scrapped," an interesting description which may have referred to an unsold remainder from some printer's or lithographer's dustbin. Those bidders feeling insufficient from the standpoint of formal education may have found Lot 89, four unspecified diplomas, to be interesting, but probably not too much so, for the entire lot brought just 12 cents.

Numismatists at the sale presumably could go out for afternoon tea, for it was not until Lot 101 that coins and tokens were offered. Under the sub-heading "Coins, Tokens, Etcetera," appeared among other items, Lot 101 Spiel Munze ("play money"), three pieces, Uncirculated, which sold for 26 cents each; Lot 103, two examples of "Sharpless & Mulligan's Card," at 26 cents each; Lot 104, two examples of "Lovett's Small Nickel Cards," likewise 26 cents each, four specimens of Washington tokens (Lot 108) at one cent each, a Hard Times token, Lot 116 described as "Loco Foco Mint Drop" at three cents, and a whole raft of political tokens (Lot 118) at two cents each.

Regular U.S. Mint coins commenced with Lot 121, a 1793 Wreath large cent, curiously described as "small, good, scarce." What was small about it? It was not stated. In any event the coin sold for 45 cents. Another 1793 Wreath cent was described as "large" and brought 50 cents. Two 1793 Chain cents, stated to be in Poor preservation, fetched 15 cents each.

Lots 148 and 149 consisted of several examples of the 1804 "restrike" cent described as being "bright." These brought 35c for one pair and 30c for another pair. Many later large cents—read this and weep—*in Uncirculated* grade sold for 3c to 15c each!

Among later items in the sale, half cents of 1833, 1834, 1835, 1849, 1850, 1851, 1853, 1854, 1855, 1856, and 1857, again each in Uncirculated grade, brought two cents each, while a small hoard (six pieces) of 1851-O Uncirculated three-cent pieces brought five cents each, and a bunch of 1860 Uncirculated three-cent silver coins brought the same price each, and an 1837 Feuchtwanger cent fetched six cents.

If one of your great-grandparents had attended the sale of 1870 and had spent, say $10 on selected items and had bequeathed them to you, you could cash in for several hundred thousand dollars today! Such is the fun of reading old auction catalogues.

Seeking to learn more about the sale and what happened there, I turned to John W. Adams' *Numismatic Literature,* Volume 1, and found that the only entry under Birch was in reference to certain auctions conducted during the period by Ebenezer Locke Mason. Likewise *The American Journal of Numismatics,* published by the American Numismatic Society, noted several sales held during 1870 and early 1871, but the December 28th offering by Thos. Birch & Son was not among them.

From Rare Coin Review No. 48, June-July 1983.

Numismatic Horoscope

By Q. David Bowers   1983

Gemini (May 21 - June 21). A chance remark at a coin club meeting may lead to a reinvestigation of the possibilities of the 1955 "Bugs Bunny" half dollar variety. Use the summer to get some exercise, but try to avoid mosquitoes. Will the new *Guide Book*, due out in July, show a sharp increase for Vermont copper coins (and might it be wise to buy two or three)?

Cancer (June 22 - July 22). A pretty face in a photograph of a crowd of auction bidders printed in *Numismatic News* has the potential for romance. Avoid buying or selling gold on the 4th of July; instead, meditate by staring at a Liberty Seated coin all day, preferably one dated 1876. Beware of a friend offering you for cash only, no receipt, an 1885-CC silver dollar.

Leo (July 23 - August 23). Auction season, coin style, is heating up, and it is uncertain whether 364 auctions are scheduled for August or just 363. Attend the ANA convention. An old lady next door has a pile of Chapman catalogues and says her grandpa used to collect coins in the 1890s; be especially nice to her. Resolve to read every word in *Coin World,* but set aside 23 days for this purpose (which means you miss reading the next two issues).

Virgo (August 24 - September 22). Study carefully any 1776 Massachusetts copper coins or 1855 Blake & Co. $20 pieces offered. A letter written to W. Elliot Woodward is returned marked "No longer at this address."

Libra (September 23 - October 23). Avoid Geminis who flatter you by saying you undergrade, when really all they are doing is seeking to buy bargains. Coin boxes in Pac-Man and Zaxxon games may be a good place to find pre-1964 silver coins; cultivate the friendship of an arcade owner. New Orleans Mint Morgan dollars look cheap.

Scorpio (October 24 - November 21). Lay in a supply of logs and numismatic books (especially *Penny Whimsy* and as many back issues of *The Numismatic Scrapbook Magazine* as you can find) for the winter, or else go to Florida and get some rest before all of the January conventions. Avoid buying coins picturing horses until after November 15th. Invite a numismatic friend, preferably of the opposite sex, over to help figure out your pasta-making machine.

Sagittarius (November 22 - December 21). Beware of market tipsters who suggest unloading your Fugio cents; instead hold, they will probably go higher, especially if the *Wall Street Journal* prints a front-page story about them. Take a magnifying glass to a game of penny-ante poker; chances are good of finding a 1972 Doubled Die cent, especially if you live in Texas, Colorado, or the Upper Peninsula of Michigan. Learn how to pronounce "Cointreau" properly.

Capricorn (December 22 - January 19). See if you can come up with a letter to the editor of *The Numismatist* about the Olympic coin designs that is different from the 1,472 opinions already printed. Buying for $3 a copy of the 1878 Mint Report at a flea market gives you a new perspective on the Morgan dollar; keep it quiet and don't tell others. Find a 1937 B. Max Mehl catalogue in your attic and scold your mother for not cashing in her life's savings back then and ordering one of everything.

Aquarius (January 20 - February 18). Reread your *Rare Coin Review* copies for the past year to see if they are worth subscribing to. Complain to your favorite coin dealer that he should have pushed you to start a type set months ago. Sell your 1955 "Bugs Bunny" halves and reinvest the proceeds in 1939 doubled Monticello nickels in VF grade. A friend may offer you a 1947 *Guide Book* for $145, but remember the prices are out of date.

Pisces (February 19 - March 20). Eschew Librans who proclaim they are especially fair about grading and have their own private grading system which isn't disclosed and which no one can figure out; the Gem BU 1892-S silver dollar at $2,000 might not be a bargain after all. Beware of Aquarians who offer circulated Susan B. Anthony dollars in investment packages. See how many investment claims you can find in numismatic periodicals, and stop at 2,500 different claims or 48 hours of effort, whichever occurs first.

Aries (March 21 - April 19). Ask someone exactly what the Garrett Collection was back in 1979-1981, and try to find a hardbound set of catalogues. Diet tip: spend lunch hours operating a Scan-O-Matic machine rather than eating. Don't fall for coin improvement kits containing wire brushes, toothpaste, sandpaper, and shoe polish.

Taurus (April 20 - May 20). Consider building a new set of shelves to store your ever-growing file of Bowers and Merena auction catalogues and *Rare Coin Reviews,* unless your spouse/lover says that throwing them away is a better idea. If you live near the Columbia River, in the Mesabi Range area, near Winslow Crater, or within a 45-minute drive of Lake Okeechobee, then you may be surprised by a commemorative half dollar find early in May. Avoid storing paper money near Bermuda onions. Be serious about numismatics, but don't forget to have a good time!

From Rare Coin Review *No. 48, June-July 1983.*

Index